The Public Speaking Bible 2024

[3 in 1] Become a Pro Public Speaker by Developing Self-Confidence on Stage and Overcoming Social Anxiety to Deliver Your Audience Memorable, Persuasive Speeches

By
Max L. Hall

Contents

Introduction

Regardless of who we are – entrepreneurs, teachers, students – each of us holds deep within our own powerful story. These are the stories of how we overcame challenges, persevered in the face of adversity, and dealt with our own self-doubt and fear. Speaking of these very personal journeys is how we connect most deeply with one another. That is why I have made it my life's work to help others find their voice through public speaking.

My own discovery of the power and joy of public speaking began in college. I was painfully shy as a child and suffered from immense stage fright well into my late teens. Even the thought of raising my hand in a small seminar class filled me with dread. However, that began to change when I took a public speaking course in my second year of university. I will never forget my first speech. My hands trembled so violently I could barely hold my notes and I experienced such an intense adrenaline rush that it culminated in a wave of nausea just before I stepped to the lectern. Yet, as I began to speak – to share just a glimpse of my own internal story – the fear slipped away. I looked out into the eyes of my audience and saw empathy and understanding shining back at me. The power of my own voice began to emerge and from that moment on, I was hooked on public speaking.

Rather than avoid my fears, I faced them directly by speaking often and seeking out opportunities to address audiences large and small. My degrees in Communication Studies focused squarely on persuasion, rhetoric, and public address. As I delved into the world of communication, I realized that I not only loved speaking myself, but also helping others overcome their own barriers to finding their voice. That is how my role as a public speaking coach and, now, author came to be.

As I reflect on that fearful young man 10 years ago, I am astonished at the journey that brought me here. But it is not my own growing fame that moves me. Rather it is the transformation I have witnessed in my students and clients.

Tamara was a highly educated engineer who swore she would never be able to present her innovative ideas due to her debilitating phobia of public speaking. Rodrigo, an inner-city high school student, believed his voice could never make a difference in his community. Sarah, who struggled all her life to make even the smallest talk in a social group shied away from anything that brought attention to herself.

Yet, in all of these cases, with time, compassion, and practical skill-building, I witnessed incredible breakthroughs. Tamara now speaks with confidence to rooms full of experts. Rodrigo rallied his peers to approach their local congressman and enact local change. And Sarah has found the power of storytelling and become a professional speaker herself. Of all my achievements, enabling others to raise their voice is by far my proudest.

Too many of us doubt our own ability to speak, or believe that what we have to offer is insignificant. We bury our voices and stories without realizing the unique power they hold. It is these personal narratives that touch people's hearts and open their minds. The art of public speaking is in unlocking that potent force hidden within you.

Whether your audience is one person or one hundred, every human has something insightful and impactful to say. And the world needs to hear it. Your story has the possibility to change lives, influence opinions, motivate action, and inspire change. But the only way that can happen is if you share it.

And it begins with you: the reader who has been drawn to this book and to its message of empowerment. My greatest hope is that together over the coming pages we crack open the last of those self-limiting beliefs that hold you back. With practical tools and emotional support, I will be your public speaking Sherpa, guiding you step-by-step to find and harness your one-of-a-kind voice.

The path is there for the taking and so very worthwhile. A world of opportunity and connection awaits beyond your comfort zone. Those applauding audiences and captive interviewers are not illusions but real possibilities for you. Your distinct story, experiences, and perspective are needed. So, let us begin now unlocking your inner public speaking potential together. The journey starts not with 10,000 people at a podium but with one voice discovering its power in front of one listener. All you need is the courage to speak and someone willing to hear you.

PART 1

The Essential Toolkit

CHAPTER 1

The Art of Public Speaking

Public speaking is both an art and a skill that involves connecting with an audience and effectively communicating ideas. Mastering public speaking requires developing a command of verbal and nonverbal techniques to captivate listeners and convey messages memorably. This chapter will provide a deep dive into the significance, evolution, and key pillars of the art of public speaking.

Understanding the Significance of Public Speaking

Public speaking is an incredibly valuable skill with many benefits across personal, professional, academic, and civic contexts. This section will take a comprehensive look at why mastering public speaking is so important and how it can enhance an individual's life, career, confidence, leadership capabilities, and ability to impact the world.

Expanding Career Opportunities

Strong public speaking skills provide a significant advantage in job hunting, promotion seeking, entrepreneurship, and navigating career changes. Speaking well in front of others is a universal asset with tangible professional benefits.

Excellence in Interviews

Interviewing for a new job or promotion relies heavily on public speaking competence. Being able to articulate experience and qualifications confidently helps candidates stand out. Answering questions thoughtfully and coherently under pressure is paramount. Conveying enthusiasm through verbal and nonverbal communication makes a strong impression. Applicants with polished public speaking chops have an edge.

Success in Sales

Sales roles demand excellent public speaking talent. Successful sales require capturing attention, building rapport, explaining benefits persuasively, overcoming objections, and closing deals through verbal skills. Skilled salespeople use storytelling, Humor, listening skills, vocal modulation, and customized presentations to meet each client's needs and priorities. Public speaking is the lifeblood of sales excellence.

Excellence in Teaching and Training

Teachers, trainers, and corporate educators rely on public speaking skills to transmit information compellingly. Lesson planning entails organizing thoughts for oral delivery to engage varied learners. Clear explanations, memorable examples, and lively delivery are essential. Public speaking ability allows teachers to inspire students and trainers to sharpen teams.

Standout Performance in Client-Facing Roles

Positions involving ongoing client relations call for public speaking proficiency to foster trust, present solutions, explain processes, resolve concerns, and serve clients. Speaking skills to explain financial matters, simplify complex issues, handle objections, and describe services help account managers, consultants, IT professionals, and many others succeed.

Opportunity in Public Life and Politics

Politics and public life are arenas where public speaking power confers massive advantages. Leadership campaigns, party functions, governance, policy advocacy, and public relations require connecting through speech. Those able to stir emotions, build consensus, and win trust through oratory often prevail in the public sphere.

Entrepreneurial Success

Entrepreneurs depend critically on public speaking skills to secure funding, lure talent, build partnerships, attract customers, and promote their vision. Pitching ideas to investors, boards, and partners requires inspirational, persuasive communication. Public speaking empowers entrepreneurs' rise.

Building Leadership Presence

Beyond career advancement, public speaking cultivates an executive presence that establishes credibility and gravitas as a leader. Speaking masterfully in front of groups or individuals is a hallmark of leaders who generate devotion and drive exceptional results.

Inspiring Teams

Great leaders tap into public speaking skills to inspire teams. They build morale, celebrate wins, offer perspective on setbacks, and communicate vision through powerful speech. Their charisma and confidence as speakers stimulate the group's shared purpose and identity. Inspiring leaders speak from the heart.

Persuading Change

Leaders leverage public speaking prowess to persuade organizations to adopt changes through rational and emotional appeal. Explaining the rationale while connecting on a values level brings others to embrace change. Their ability to articulate complex ideas and respond impromptu helps them carry the day.

Training and Teaching

Exceptional leaders often serve as chief teachers and trainers within their organizations through public speaking. They ensure understanding, transmit culture, provide feedback, promote development, and build capabilities through clear instructional communication. Their mastery as speakers enables teaching at scale.

Crisis Response

Inevitable crises require leaders to communicate difficult news, maintain poise, offer reassurance, and provide direction through speech. Leaders without public speaking ability often flounder amidst crises. Strong speakers provide stability. Their verbal confidence inspires collective calm and focus when it matters most.

Modeling Organizational Values

Through daily communication, leadership presence originates from authentically modeling values like integrity, accountability, inclusion, and growth. Leaders who speak honestly and relatably inspire teams to embrace the organization's purpose and principles. Public speaking provides the platform for leaders' values to shape culture.

Building Partnerships

Thriving organizations require leaders who build partnerships through effective communication. Leaders open doors, foster goodwill, negotiate win-win arrangements, resolve conflicts, and promote collaboration through interpersonal public speaking skills. Their ability to find common ground through speech is invaluable.

Influencing People and Events

Beyond business and organizational contexts, public speaking has enormous power to inform perspectives, change minds, and drive historical events on a societal level. Great speakers transform attitudes, further cause, and shape history.

Shaping Public Opinion

Skilled public speakers are outsized in moving public opinion through emotionally compelling and intellectually penetrating communication. Their soaring oratory and substance can turn tides of social sentiment on issues from civil rights to climate change. They bring audiences along through eloquence.

Catalyzing Social Change

From Moses to Dr. King, transformational speakers have electrified movements and catalyzed social change. Their words mobilize people toward purposeful collective action. Speeches celebrate community, highlight injustice, and bond diverse voices to generate an unstoppable swell. Change makers speak change into being.

Countering Harmful Narratives

Public speaking has huge potential to counter false or harmful narratives that take hold within societies. Speaking truth to misinformation and hate spreads light into darkness. Courageous speakers replace lies with human truth through speech. They rewrite vicious narratives through simple humanity.

Preserving and Reclaiming Culture

Oral storytelling and public speech preserve cultural memory and reclaim lost or suppressed cultural identity. The spoken word passes traditions between generations. It reminds people who they are at their core and blooms pride in their heritage. Public speaking keeps culture alive.

Promoting Beneficial Policies and Ideas

Skilled speakers can immensely promote crucial policies, frameworks, and ideas to realize a better world. Their rhetorical gifts can make complex solutions understandable and moving to general audiences. Public speaking drives progress on poverty, education, conservation, and more.

Bringing Ideas and Passion to Life

Public speaking represents the most powerful and immediate way for human beings to translate ideas, feelings, and experiences to one another. Speaking allows logic and emotion to resonate in a profound heart-to-heart communication channel.

Tangibility Through Voice

Spoken language gives ideas and stories tangible life unachievable through writing alone. The human voice's textures, rhythms, tones, and pacing create unique vividness. Great orators make words shimmer with possibility, and imagination grips listeners. Speaking makes language human.

Evoking Emotion

Speech facilitates profoundly emotional communication through the voice's expressiveness. Stirring narratives, Humor, poetic phrases, and pregnant pauses spur emotional transportation when spoken. Audiences laugh, tear up, swell with hope, burn with conviction, and absorb ideas on a heart level, thanks to intonation and delivery.

Nuance and Emphasis

Spoken communication allows orators to improvise emphasis and subtle nuances that are impossible to note on paper. Great speakers raise and lower their voices for dramatic effect, speed up and slow down strategically, and use pregnant pauses to underscore key ideas. These flourishes rivet audiences and enrich meaning.

Storytelling's Rhythms

When told orally, stories draw power from rhythm, repetition, and audience participation. Call and response, refrains, chanting, and song punctuate the narrative when spoken live. The storyteller gauges reactions and adjusts pacing accordingly. These live rhythms forge community and memory.

Nonverbal Communication

Facial expressions, hand gestures, stances, and other nonverbal cues allow speakers to communicate additional meaning and emotion beyond words. Emphatic nonverbals enhance understanding, convey personality, and help audiences visualize ideas. Public speaking integrates verbal and nonverbal channels.

Feedback and Audience Energy

Live public speaking enables audience reactions and feedback to shape the speech experience. Through laughter, applause, body language, or vocalizations, listeners signal their engagement and guide the speaker. This live feedback loop focuses on communicative energy.

Strengthening Critical Thinking

Preparing and presenting public speeches fosters rigorous critical thinking skills for organizing and communicating information clearly and persuasively. These cognitive abilities to analyze, synthesize, and evaluate content translate widely beyond public speaking contexts.

Evaluating Source Material

Public speaking requires determining source credibility, identifying faulty logic, spotting cherry-picked data, and weighing evidence. Analyzing reference material to craft speeches strengthens the ability to evaluate information analytically. Speakers learn to separate truth from manipulation.

Synthesizing Coherently

Organizing disparate facts and ideas into coherent narratives demands synthesis and summary. Speakers must distill mountains of material into concise key points for time-bound speeches. This necessitates strong comprehension and synthesis abilities.

Logical Structuring

Speeches require logical flow and sequencing to build understanding across sections and transitions. Structuring a speech involves spatial thinking to map informational cause-and-effect and hierarchical relationships. Crafting logical structure strengthens systems analysis capabilities.

Persuasive Reasoning

Public speaking prioritizes rational appeals over pure emotion. Effective persuasion requires airtight, logical reasoning to change hearts and minds. The intellectual discipline needed for persuasive speeches translates directly to rhetorical skills in writing and debate.

Mental Composure

Speaking off notes or impromptu in front of others requires mental composure to think on one's feet. Public speaking builds self-discipline and stress tolerance to marshal thoughts clearly under pressure. This develops grace under fire.

Communication Excellence

Preparing speeches elevates broader communication abilities. It builds skills for translating complex concepts into simpler terms, creating vivid analogies, enhancing explanations, and tailoring messaging to different audiences. Public speaking is a microcosm for overall communication excellence.

Overcoming Challenges and Building Confidence

Public speaking requires moving beyond limitations and discomfort to unlock latent potential. Growth comes from getting outside your comfort zone and doing what once seemed daunting. Each speech completed builds confidence to take on greater challenges beyond public speaking contexts.

Managing Anxiety

Anxiety about public performance is nearly universal. Pushing through this fear to speak successfully helps reframe how the brain responds to nerve-inducing situations. Meeting the challenge repatterns thinking of anxiety as excitement to harness rather than a reason to avoid.

Unlocking Potential

Fulfilling the role of speaker or performer involves projecting confidence even when unsure and drawing on courage beyond everyday limits. Preparing and delivering speeches taps into latent layers of charisma, gravitas, and capability within each person. Speaking grows self-belief.

Handling Exposure

Speaking publicly entails increased visibility and exposure. Managing emotions builds the capacity to handle being seen and heard. Getting comfortable with exposure develops emotional resilience and reduces overinvestment in external judgment. Growth comes from moving beyond self-consciousness.

Releasing Perfectionism

Great public speaking requires releasing perfectionistic urges to control reactions and feel certain before acting. Speeches never turn out exactly as planned. This reality motivates developing great improvisation skills and learning to thrive amid uncertainty. Letting go opens possibilities.

Enjoying the Experience

Each public speech completed reinforces confidence and a taste for the experience. The sense of contribution, growth, and enhanced connection with audiences builds intrinsic motivation. Speaking ceases being intimidating and becomes profoundly rewarding. Fears evolve into appreciation of a special opportunity.

The Historical Evolution of Public Speaking

Public speaking has evolved across cultures and eras alongside the progression of human civilization. Tracing its historical development reveals the enduring significance of oral communication in teaching, leading, persuading, and forging bonds among humanity. Examining this rich heritage provides important context, insights, and lessons for aspiring speakers today.

Foundations in Ancient Greece and Rome

Formal public speaking traces back to ancient Greek democracy, where engaged citizens debated issues and shaped opinions through speeches. Renowned thinkers like Socrates, Plato, and Aristotle analyzed persuasion and spoke before gatherings.

In Roman society, Cicero and others refined eloquent oratory. Principles like logos, ethos, and pathos were established, and rhetorical education was formalized. This Greco-Roman tradition of rhetoric hugely influenced later public speaking's development.

Greek Rhetorical Schools

Ancient Greece generated the first formal schools of rhetorical education, with sophists teaching persuasive speaking techniques for civic life.

Aristotle's Rhetoric analyzed modes of persuasion that are still instructive today. Philosophers like Isocrates pioneered rhetorical principles for amplification, style, and delivery. Greek oratory competitions honed skills.

Roman Legal and Political Rhetoric

Roman speakers like Cicero demonstrated the power of eloquence to influence legal proceedings and senate debates.

Cicero's techniques for graceful delivery, emotional appeal, and ethical persuasion remain pertinent. Distinguished Roman orators proved speech's ability to shape thoughts and drive collective action.

Greco-Roman Theatre and Performance

In ancient Greece and Rome, stage performances and rituals established important performative elements of public speaking like vocal projection, expressive delivery, audience engagement, and integration of nonverbal communication. Dramatic conventions influenced speech presentation.

Development of Rhetoric as a Civic Art

Classical rhetoric established public speaking as a recognized civic discipline. Proficiency was seen as a duty and virtue for participation in democracy. Core principles still apply regarding proper structuring of arguments, appeals to reason and emotion, style, and memory techniques. This conception of rhetoric elevated oratory in culture.

Decline of Public Speech in the Middle Ages

The Middle Ages saw a decline in public speaking as written texts and manuscripts gained primacy. Church authority emphasized Scripture over crowdspeaking. Political assemblies and democratic forums faded. However, some key traditions enabled later revival.

Primacy of Written Scripture

Christian theology and church scholasticism shifted focus toward biblical interpretation and preaching based on Scripture. Public speech became less tied to civic life. Written language and texts gained cultural power, while most remained illiterate.

Decline of Democratic Assemblies

Feudalism displaced participatory civic forums of the classical era. Lords and vassals interacted through written proclamations rather than speeches. Democratic rhetoric skills faded without public venues for open debate between citizens and shaping collective will.

Preservation in Church Preaching

While public speech waned in politics and society, oral performance lived on through priests' sermons in church. Rhetorical skills applied to preaching biblical lessons. This preserved public speaking for sacred purposes as secular venues diminished.

Monastic Manuscripts and Writings

Monasteries meticulously copied and stored ancient Greek and Roman rhetorical writings and manuals. This preserved foundational public speaking knowledge through the Middle Ages until its rediscovery in the Renaissance. Manuscript circulation kept rhetoric concepts alive.

Oral Folk Narratives and Epic Poems

Vibrant oral storytelling traditions maintained a bridge to more conversational and performance-based speech. Legends, folk tales, epic poems, and ballads passed through live recitals, building community between generations. Such storytelling kept direct oral communication prevalent outside official church doctrine.

Resurgence of Rhetoric in Renaissance Europe

The rediscovery of classical philosophy and education starting in the 14th century European Renaissance rekindled interest in rhetorical communication. Oratory reemerged as an academic discipline and cultural marker of erudition. Developments set the stage for public speaking's wide use.

Revival of Greek and Roman writings

Thinkers revived Greco-Roman rhetorical works preserved in monastery libraries. Translations made Cicero, Quintilian, Aristotle, and others' writings widely available. This resurrected ancient theories on structuring and delivering speeches. Public speaking reentered mainstream education.

Growing Civic Arenas for Public Speech

Emerging merchant class forums, early legislative assemblies, universities, and expanded trade created secular venues for public speaking beyond just the pulpit. More opportunities arose to speak persuasively on secular matters like politics, philosophy, and community affairs.

Codification in disciplinary Handbooks

Influential manuals like Erasmus's "On Copia of Words and Ideas" provided humanist instruction on rhetorical composition and eloquent expression, reconnecting to ancient traditions. These handbooks disseminated speechmaking principles and spread structured approaches to preparing orations.

Emphasis on Style and Delivery

Renaissance oratory prized elements like articulate voice, physical grace and posture, stylistic flourish, and dramatically paced delivery. Ideals for oral style and presentation were gleaned from ancient writers like Cicero and Quintilian. Polished delivery is defined as refined speech.

Rhetoric as Civic and Moral Virtue

Renaissance thinkers framed rhetoric and public speech as civic duties and moral virtues. Eloquence signaled wisdom, and silence signified the surrender of social responsibility. Speechmaking ability marked engaged citizenship. Oratory became a hallmark of humanistic learning and character.

Public Speaking's Flowering in Modern Democracy

The 17th-19th centuries saw public speaking assume a central role in political and cultural life thanks to new educational venues, democratic reforms, and breakthrough technologies enabling communication at scale. Speaking skills now conferred substantial public influence.

Rhetoric as a Core Academic Discipline

Modern colleges and universities made rhetoric, and oratory established academic fields. Students studied classical texts and gave practice orations. Professors like Scottish elocutionists trained lawyers, ministers, and politicians. Public speaking was considered vital preparation for leadership.

Rise of Legislative Oratory

In nations like Britain and revolutionary America, elected parliaments and assemblies rose as platforms for prominent political speeches. Debates in these bodies enabled affecting policy through public speaking prowess, as practiced by leaders like Edmund Burke, Henry Clay, and Daniel Webster.

Growth of Lyceum Movement

Widespread public education and enlarged leisure time catalyzed the American lyceum movement, featuring lectures on moral, civic, and scientific topics. Celebrated speakers like Ralph Waldo Emerson, Susan B. Anthony, and Mark Twain lectured before community gatherings nationwide.

Advances in Print Media and Literacy

Wider literacy, cheaper printing, and expansive newspapers and pamphlets accelerated the printed dissemination of major speeches by leading orators. Print coverage amplified reach and impact, fueling public speaking's relevance and renown.

Technological Amplification of Voice

New amplification technologies like miniature megaphones and PA systems overcame biological limits on speech volume, enabling large outdoor and indoor audiences. Radio broadcasts transmitted famous voices like Huey Long and Franklin Roosevelt into every home.

Public Speaking in The Contemporary Digital Landscape

Television, internet video, online communities, and interactive multimedia have transformed public speaking, creating new challenges and possibilities for making an enduring impact. Digital tools have expanded access and data while threatening to diminish oral communication's immediacy.

Rise of Online Video Platforms

YouTube, TED, Facebook Live, podcasts, and others enable speeches to reach global digital audiences. Distribution barriers have vanished. However, the impersonal digital space often lacks live spoken communication's dynamism and feedback.

Data Analytics' Double Edge

Digital metrics provide data on views, clicks, and audience demographics. But obsessive analytics threaten to reduce public speaking to formulas. Authentic human connection exceeds quantifiable data. The danger arises from optimizing speeches for metrics over meaning.

The Proliferation of Online Communities

Digital groups united by shared interests foster specialized public speaking to engage niche audiences. This fragmentation makes uniting broad, varied audiences behind unifying messages more difficult than in previous mass communication eras.

Multimedia Speech Visual Integration

Modern public speaking adopts slide presentations, infographics, embedded video clips, and other visual elements owing to short digital attention spans. The risk is an overreliance on slides weakens speechwriting craft. Multimedia should amplify, not substitute for, skillful oral communication.

Resurgent Appraisal of Intimate Speech

Even amidst digital saturation, intimate communal speaking formats like storytelling slams, neighborhood potlucks, and discussion circles have flourished. People crave personal connection conveyed through the living spoken word. Intimate speech persists despite technology.

Overview of the Three Key Pillars

Public speaking mastery relies on competency across three foundational pillars: 1) Core speaking skills, 2) Subject matter command, and 3) Mental and physical presentation. Proficiency requires blended development across these pillars into a unified practice. This section will survey the key elements of each.

Core Speaking Skills

Certain speechmaking abilities are the basic toolbox for translating ideas and content into dynamic oral presentations. Core skills consist of:

Speech Organization

Logical structure and sequencing allow listeners to absorb ideas. Key elements are the introduction, body, and conclusion. Transitions should connect sections smoothly. Strong organization entails highlighting themes, marshaling supporting points, and building toward a unified message.

Crafting Solid Content

Content forms the substance of any speech. Effective speakers research their topics extensively to craft well-informed speeches with accuracy, depth, and insight. Points should be concise yet rich with facts, examples, anecdotes, and explanations to create an interesting informational experience.

Storytelling Techniques

Storytelling makes speeches relatable, memorable, and impactful. Stories should have a clear arc and evocative details without rambling. Dialogue, tension, and descriptive language should transport listeners into the story's world. Personal narratives, historical stories, and literary allusions have great power.

Rhetorical Techniques

Devices like metaphors, analogies, triplets, contrasts, and repetition build eloquence. Word play through alliteration, assonance, and consonance also enlivens language. Rhetorical questions, exclamations, and syncopated phrasing punctuate speeches for rhetorical flair.

Conversational Tone

Conversational language leverages familiar, everyday words and expressions for intimate communication. Short sentences and simple syntax relate directly to listeners. First and second-person point of view fosters a friendly tone and rapport. The speech still develops complexity but through plainspoken language.

Vocal Techniques

Modulating pitch, pace, volume, and tone keeps audiences engaged. Short punctuating phrases should be spoken loudly and slowly. Whispering or singing certain words calls attention to them. Pausing for dramatic or comedic effect builds anticipation. Vocal techniques amplify meaning.

Nonverbal Communication

Gestures like pointing, pantomiming, and open palms reinforce speech visually. Moving around the stage rather than remaining static adds kinesthetic energy. Posture, stance, and facial expressions help connect with listeners. Nonverbal elements complement the verbal message.

Command of Subject Matter

Authoritative speeches require expertise in the topic developed through extensive study, research, and analysis. Deep subject matter command includes:

Grasping Historical Context

Understanding how current issues and concepts evolved historically allows a richer exploration of origins and causality. Background enriches the explanation of present significance. Speakers should anchor topics in historical forces and milestones.

Mastering Philosophical Foundations

For conceptual topics, grasping philosophical underpinnings, theories, and seminal thinkers equips speakers to analyze issues incisively. Speakers should interpret subjects through philosophical lenses like ethics, epistemology, and metaphysics.

Fluency with Principal Research

Familiarity with academic and scientific research methodologies like peer review, controlled variables, statistical significance, and research ethics allows for discerning evaluation of findings authority. Speakers should emphasize only rigorous, unbiased research.

Immersion in Facts and Data

Factual accuracy and illustrative data are great speechmaking assets. But facts should be verified across reputable sources, not cherry-picked to confirm biases. Data is strongest through visualization tools like charts showing trends. Immersion in details makes speeches multidimensional.

Synthesis of Disparate Elements

Synthesizing interconnected elements into unified narratives requires deep understanding. For example, grasping how poetry, music, and visual art intersect as creative expressions. Making conceptual connections conveys true mastery.

Comprehension of Complex Systems

Whether natural systems like ecosystems or human constructs like markets, understanding complex wholes facilitates explaining interdependencies and relationships among components, and a grasp of systems enables articulating how each part matters to the greater entity.

Mental and Physical Presentation

Public speaking excellence relies on mental and physical disciplines around self-awareness, confidence, preparation, and performance. Strong presentation stems from:

Managing Anxiety

Anxiety is natural. Preparation rituals, power poses, positive self-talk, and reframing anxiety as excitement help channel nerves productively. Getting experience builds confidence. The goal is acknowledging anxiety without judgment and preventing inhibition.

Authentic Passion and Enthusiasm

Passion for the topic is contagious. When speakers exude genuine excitement, audiences become invested. Avoiding monotonous delivery and infusing energy into the face, voice, and body language expresses infectious enthusiasm. Passion brings speeches fully to life.

Meticulous Preparation

Practice and rehearsal elevate speeches through timing refinement, smooth sequencing, and nuanced delivery. Outlining provides structure while allowing flexibility. Internalizing a few lead sentences for each section enables improvisation around the main ideas. Meticulous preparation instills confidence and rapport.

Immersive Memorization

Total memorization frees speakers from notes to connect with audiences. But memorization should arise organically from immersion in the speech's logical flow and meaning, not just rote lines. Thorough familiarity with the material makes recall natural.

Attention to Posture and Movement

Good posture projects confidence and opens the diaphragm for full breathing. Efficient movement around the stage maintains audience engagement without distracting fidgeting. Hands should convey meaning, not nervous energy. Physical presence impacts audience connection.

Mindfulness of Habits and Distractions

Noticing unconscious mannerisms like ums, ahs, and ticks allows speakers to minimize distractions. Any idiosyncrasies should be reframed as deliberate choices. Mindfulness of habits prevents disconnecting from audiences.

Vulnerability and Courage

Speaking authentically requires the courage to share oneself and risk judgments. Speakers should reveal passion and humanity freely. Living the content makes it compelling. Willing vulnerability forges profound speaker-audience bonds.

When integrated, these three pillars erect the foundation for public speaking excellence. They enable translating ideas and passion into speeches that educate, inspire, and empower audiences.

CHAPTER 2
Building Self-Confidence

Self-confidence is essential for effective public speaking. When we lack self-confidence, we become preoccupied with self-doubt and are likelier to make mistakes. In contrast, we can focus fully on our message and audience when we have self-confidence. As the famous Dale Carnegie quote goes: "Develop success from failures. Discouragement and failure are two of the surest steppingstones to success." This chapter provides strategies and techniques to help develop the self-confidence required to become an accomplished public speaker.

Identifying Sources of Self-Doubt

Social Anxiety

Social anxiety is one of the most common sources of self-doubt when it comes to public speaking. This refers to excessive fear or nervousness regarding social situations, especially when others evaluate or judge one. Physical symptoms of social anxiety include a racing heart, sweating, shaking, and upset stomach. Cognitive symptoms include negative self-talk such as "I'm going to mess up" or "The audience will think I'm stupid." Social anxiety can significantly impact one's ability to speak confidently in front of others. The first step is acknowledging if social anxiety is an issue. From there, one can use strategies in this chapter to manage it.

Negative Past Experiences

Past public speaking experiences where we made mistakes or were criticized can erode self-confidence. These negative experiences get imprinted in our minds, causing apprehension. For instance, if you completely blanked out during a high school presentation, the memory could instill self-doubt years later. Or if you were ridiculed for mispronouncing a word in a previous speech, you may question your abilities. To build confidence, reflect on past negative experiences objectively. Recognize that poor speech does not define your abilities. We all make mistakes—focus on learning rather than lamenting. Believe in your ability to improve.

Imposter Syndrome

Many competent individuals suffer from imposter syndrome—the persistent fear of being exposed as a fraud or incapable. Despite proven abilities, they doubt their competence and fear others will eventually unmask their inadequacy. Public speaking can amplify this feeling when we worry about being critiqued. To overcome imposter syndrome, recognize that these thoughts are irrational and false. You do have the skills and knowledge to succeed in public speaking. Focus on preparing well rather than worrying you might be "found out."

Fear of Judgment

Fear of being negatively evaluated is another source of self-doubt. We may worry about being judged for a poor speech performance, a boring topic, a silly mistake, or simply being ourselves. But the audience wants you to succeed—they are rooting for you. Avoid catastrophizing and making faulty mind-reading assumptions about their opinions. Stay focused on your message rather than perceived judgments. Also, remember that people tend to be distracted and focus less on evaluating you.

Comparisons to Others

It's easy to undermine confidence by comparing ourselves to other speakers who seem more eloquent, experienced, or comfortable. But these comparisons are usually skewed. We see other's public personas but not their private struggles. Recognize your unique strengths, and don't judge yourself by other's standards. With practice, you can also reach higher levels of proficiency. Believe in your potential for growth.

Imposed Self-Doubt

Sometimes, self-doubt is imposed on us by outside criticism that gets internalized over time. A thoughtless comment from a past teacher, aside from a peer, or outright public speaking shaming can undermine confidence. Recognize these past incidents were more a reflection of the critic than your capability. Let go of those distorted opinions. Isolated comments of others do not determine your skills and worth. You are capable of improving with each speech.

Self-Confidence Building Strategies

Positive Affirmations and Self-Talk

Words carry power. What we repeatedly tell ourselves shapes our self-perception and confidence. When gearing up for a speech, avoid dwelling on anxious self-talk such as, "I'm going to mess this up so bad." Instead, intentionally cultivate positive self-affirmations such as "I am prepared and will deliver an engaging speech." Speak words of confidence to drown out self-doubt. Post motivational quotes and affirmations around your home. Repeat statements like "I am capable and poised" while getting ready to reinforce confidence. Over time, these positive affirmations will transform your self-belief and confidence.

Visualization Techniques

Visualization utilizes your imagination to boost confidence through mental rehearsal. By picturing yourself succeeding, you prime the mind and body for success. Begin by relaxing and imagining yourself calmly walking on stage. Visualize smiling and making eye contact as you deliver your speech smoothly and competently. Envision the audience nods and engrossed expressions. Picture the ovation at the end. Mentally rehearse the experience of your successful speech to reinforce confidence. Repeat this visualization practice regularly to cement the vision and physiological readiness for unflappable confidence.

Cognitive Behavioral Therapy (CBT) for Confidence

Cognitive behavioral therapy is an evidence-based approach that helps reframe unhelpful thought patterns. Many negative thoughts are distorted and reinforce self-doubt, so CBT helps alter thinking to be more objective. For example, replace thoughts like "I always mess up speeches" with more accurate statements such as "I have more experience now and am better prepared than in the past." CBT also involves behavioral experiments to test out the integrity of thoughts. For example, purposely make a small mistake, then assess if the worst-case scenario you feared comes true. Applying CBT can transform negative thinking that undermines confidence.

Theodore Roosevelt's Method

Theodore Roosevelt eventually overcame substantial childhood health problems to become president of the United States. He credited his success to what he called "the strenuous life." This involved continually testing one's comfort zone and building courage through practice despite fear. Roosevelt advised: "Do what you can, with what you have, where you are." Apply this to public speaking by continually stretching your abilities, such as volunteering for speeches even if you feel unready. As Roosevelt stated: "Every time you stop a bad habit, you strengthen your character a little bit." Facing fears builds confidence.

Redefining Mistakes

How we perceive mistakes also impacts confidence. Many view mistakes as failures and proof of ineptitude. But mistakes are an essential part of learning. Reframe mistakes as valuable feedback is needed for growth. Additionally, small mistakes during speeches are rarely catastrophic. Letting perfectionism breed self-doubt only hinders improvement. Strive for excellence, but not unconscious perfection. Allow yourself to make mistakes while learning from them. This growth mindset builds confidence to keep trying and improving without self-judgment.

Managing Self-Critical Thoughts

For many, the inner critic is the loudest voice undermining confidence. Self-critical thoughts like "I'm not good enough" inevitably trigger self-doubt. When those critical thoughts arise, consciously acknowledge them, then deliberately replace them with more supportive self-talk. For instance, replace "Who do you think you are? You're going to look like an idiot" with "I've prepared thoroughly and will do my best to engage the audience." Also, speak to yourself as you would a respected friend. Positive self-talk can become instinctive with practice, while self-criticism loses its grip.

Harnessing Nervous Energy

Some self-doubt stems from misinterpreting the body's normal stress response as a sign we are incapable of handling the pressure. Reframe anxiety as excitement that can give your speech power and passion. As Sami Serageldin stated, "Don't fear fear. Let it sharpen you, alarm you, and keep you awake. But don't fear it." Some nervousness provides the adrenaline to make your speech lively and memorable. Reframe nerves as energy to channel into your performance. Embrace and harness it.

Cultivating Emotional Intelligence

Emotional intelligence enables recognizing and managing emotions to think clearly under pressure. This involves identifying areas of self-doubt and then developing rational responses. For example, recognize if fear of judgment is irrational given your capabilities and preparation. Or identify when perfectionism is hindering your willingness to practice. Strategies to overcome sources of self-doubt build confidence to succeed despite inevitable setbacks. Emotional intelligence allows managing emotions, so they fuel, rather than hinder, your potential.

Setting Smaller Goals

Sometimes, the sheer scope of public speaking can seem daunting, undermining confidence in our ability to master the challenge. Restore confidence by breaking overall development into smaller, manageable goals. Focus on specific skills like crafting memorable introductions or gesturing naturally. Master them individually before combining everything required for an entire speech. Each smaller goal met provides a confidence boost to achieve the next one. Like stacking building blocks, achieving a progression of smaller goals constructs overall confidence.

Aerobic Exercise

Aerobic exercise is proven to stimulate confidence along with physical health. Activities like jogging, biking, or swimming release endorphins that boost mood and self-assurance. Increased blood and oxygen to the brain sharpens focus while reducing stress hormones. Schedule aerobic exercise into your routine to stimulate self-confidence on a physiological level. Interestingly, even exercising the morning of a speech can boost self-assurance. But consistency over the long-term provides the greatest lasting confidence gains.

Developing Resilience and Handling Setbacks

Reframing Fear of Failure

While failure can breed self-doubt, worry about failure often causes more distress than actual failure. When you fear failure, you dread the unknown versus the actual event. Remember that small failures when public speaking are usually not true disasters but learning experiences. Reframe failure as an opportunity for growth, not proof you are inadequate. View failures as isolated incidents rather than indictments of your identity. Developing a growth mindset allows resilience after minor setbacks during speeches.

Letting Go of Perfectionism

Perfectionism can corrode self-confidence when unrealistic standards are not met, which is inevitable. Polishing speeches is beneficial, but perfectionism can lead to never-ending obsessive editing. Instead, strive for excellence while avoiding unrealistic expectations that you must be flawless. Letting go of rigid perfectionism reduces self-judgment and builds resilience to deliver your best effort without demanding infallibility. Keep the perspective that the audience wants authenticity over perfection anyway. Progress, not perfection, builds confidence.

Focusing on Controllable

Low confidence often develops when dwelling on factors outside your control. We cannot control every variable, like audience size or mood. Instead, concentrate confidence on your preparation and performance. With practice, skills within your control, like content, delivery, and handling nerves, can regularly be executed well. You may not be able to dictate outcomes, but you can control your abilities. Staying focused on the controllable elements ensures you are ready to handle uncontrollable variables that arise confidently.

Maintaining Perspective

Minor public speaking mishaps can get blown out of proportion in your mind, damaging your self-confidence. Maintain perspective by realizing most speaking blunders are not catastrophes. If you accidentally mispronounce a word or phrase, correct yourself and continue your speech smoothly. The audience understands mistakes happen. Keep mishaps in perspective rather than dwell on them. Also, remember that critical self-assessments after a speech are usually distorted negatively. We are our own worst critics. Strive to evaluate performances fairly with a perspective on what went well, too.

Having Compassion

Treat yourself with the compassion you would show a respected friend in the same situation. We often unduly beat ourselves up for minor mistakes and shortcomings. Rather than harsh self-criticism, offer honest feedback with gentleness, patience, and encouragement. Identify lessons learned without judgment. Have compassion on yourself for being human rather than demanding you function perfectly under pressure. Bring the positive perspective and support you would give a friend. Compassion fosters resilience and continued progress after a setback.

Getting Back on the Horse

After a disappointing experience, the natural impulse is often avoidance. However, avoiding future public speaking only magnifies self-doubt and fear. Instead, purposefully get back out there and try again. Sign up to speak at the next opportunity. When you get back on the horse promptly, you regain the self-confidence that was shaken. Each additional successful speech, even if imperfect, builds competence to try again. As Eleanor Roosevelt advised, "Do one thing every day that scares you." Avoidance breeds self-doubt, while persistence builds resilience.

CHAPTER 3
Crafting Memorable Speeches

Delivering a memorable speech requires far more than standing up in front of an audience and sharing your thoughts. Crafting a speech that engages your listeners, imparts key messages, and leaves a lasting impression demands rigorous preparation and careful attention to detail. This chapter will provide public speaking students with strategies and best practices for structuring, supporting, and polishing speeches to maximize their impact.

We will begin by emphasizing the importance of thoroughly analyzing your audience and customizing your speech accordingly. Understanding who your listeners are, what information they need, and how to appeal to their interests is the foundation of an effective speech. Next, we will examine proven speech organizational structures, including compelling introductions and conclusions. You will learn techniques for seamlessly transitioning from point to point, keeping your speech cohesive and easy to follow.

This chapter focuses on choosing and utilizing supporting materials that reinforce your speech and boost your credibility as a speaker. We will explore how to skillfully incorporate data, statistics, research findings, quotations, anecdotes, explanations, and examples into your speech. You will also learn guidelines for creating clear, readable visual aids and seamlessly incorporating multimedia to increase audience engagement. Finally, we will discuss polishing techniques such as vocal variety, powerful word choice, and practiced delivery that transform a good speech into an exceptional one. Let's get started exploring the secrets of crafting memorable speeches!

Audience Analysis

Before you begin writing your speech, you must understand your audience. Detailed audience analysis is crucial for shaping your content, style, and delivery approach to reach your listeners effectively. The more you know about your audience's demographics, psychographics, needs, and expectations, the better you can tailor your speech to them. Thorough audience analysis enables you to craft content that resonates, present information they can easily understand, establish credibility, and motivate your listeners. This section will provide public speaking students with techniques for analyzing an audience and customizing speech content accordingly.

Understanding Audience Demographics

Your audience's demographic composition encompasses factors like age, gender, ethnicity, education level, socioeconomic status, and more. Gaining insight into demographic details helps you determine an appropriate tone for your speech, include relevant examples, and gauge listeners' potential knowledge level. For instance, a talk on retirement planning would likely vary greatly when presented to a high school audience versus a group of 60-year-olds. Pay attention to demographic factors that seem particularly relevant to your speech topic and aim to incorporate examples, explanations, and language suitable for that demographic profile. If possible, directly survey audience members beforehand using a questionnaire to gather accurate demographic information. You can also contact event organizers to request a general demographic breakdown if one is available.

Recognizing Psychographic Factors

While demographics provide useful data, psychographics give you deeper insight into your audience's attitudes, interests, values, and beliefs. Start by researching any affiliations or organizations represented in your audience.

Are they members of a political party, employees of the same company, or supporters of a particular cause? Understand what drew them to the group and which values they share. Additionally, learn what topics, issues, and pain points resonate most with this audience. Scan local newspapers, blogs, social media, and other sources to identify their concerns. Finally, notice what cultural references, celebrities, or stereotypes positively or negatively color their worldview. Tapping into psychographics lets you emphasize shared values, play to positive stereotypes, and choose examples that resonate with their interests and concerns.

Determining Audience Needs and Expectations

Beyond abstract group attributes, consider the practical needs, motivations, and expectations of the individuals and the organization assembled by your audience. Ask: why are listeners specifically attending your speech? Do they need general information about your topic or require instructions to solve a problem? Are they educated, motivated to act, sold a product, or entertained? Understanding defined needs and goals will keep your speech sharply focused.

Additionally, assess audience expectations based on the speaker, setting, and stated purpose. The expected tone, depth, and takeaways will vary for a keynote address versus a panel talk or ceremonial speech. Carefully balance required content with realistic timing constraints. Researching needs and expectations will ensure you deliver the speech your audience wants and needs to hear.

Adapting Content to Your Audience

Armed with audience insights, systematically incorporate appropriate adaptations into your speech at all levels. First, adjust your tone and language choices to align with audience demographics like age, education level, ethnicity, and background knowledge. For instance, eliminate jargon when addressing general audiences while engaging specialists with more technical details. Next, pepper in psychographic details through shared values statements, topical examples, celebrated cultural references, and witty asides that play to stereotypes. Drastically shape speech structure and emphasis based on audience needs and occasion. For instance, an awareness-building speech will dedicate more time to foundational education versus a motivation speech aiming to fire up knowledgeable supporters. Finally, meet expectations through style, length, actionable takeaways, and more. The more adjustments you make to tailor content to your listeners, the more receptive, engaged, and responsive your audience will be.

Speech Structure

While a speech should flow naturally, a strong underlying organizational structure creates an indispensable framework. The introduction, body, and conclusion format provide an organizing principle to guide content development and sequencing. Attention-grabbing openings and closings act as bookends, anchoring listeners and framing your message. Strategic transitions seamlessly stitch together pieces into a cohesive whole. This section will outline time-tested structural elements that coalesce into memorable speeches.

Crafting Strong Introductions

The introduction serves the critical functions of grabbing the audience's attention, establishing credibility and rapport, framing the speech's scope, and previewing key points. Effective openings draw distracted listeners through startling statements, Humor, questions, anecdotes, quotes, or intriguing props. For example, open with a startling fact about your speech topic or a provocative question for the audience. Briefly introduce yourself if unknown and cite qualifications that reinforce your credibility. Next, clearly state your speech's central thesis and delineate the specific scope of supporting points. Finally, provide an overview of the main points to orient the audience to your structure. Keep introductions concise but packed with compelling hooks, credibility boosters, and structural signposts audience members need to become engaged, receptive listeners.

Structuring the Body with Key Points

While introductions set the stage, speech bodies deliver a message substance through clear explanations, persuasive reasoning, and supporting evidence. Carefully select three to five key points that scaffold upward to build understanding or drive your argument forward. Devote the majority of speech time to expanding upon these points. Organize points in a logical but varied sequence; options include chronological, problem-solution, spatial, comparison, or order of importance frameworks. Limit each key point discussion to a few minutes to avoid listener fatigue. Employ transitions to guide the audience from one point to the next smoothly. Finally, incorporate varied supporting materials to illustrate, explain, or provide evidence for each point. Following a clear organizational structure allows you to convey information effectively within time constraints.

Closing with Impact

Your closing mirrors the introduction by reading the speech and hammering your message home. Effective closings begin by transitioning from the body using summary signposts and then briefly recapping main points. Avoid simply restating each key point; synthesize them into concise takeaway messages you want to resonate with after your speech concludes. Look ahead to applications, next steps, or future possibilities regarding your topic. Finally, close with a memorable final thought via an apt metaphor, pithy quote, or call to action. Maintain momentum until the last moment by ending crisply; draw out your final sentence to emphasize its significance. Strong closings reinforce central ideas and spur future thought, ensuring your speech sticks with the audience long after its conclusion.

Strengthening Flow with Transitions

Transitions are bridges that transport your audience smoothly from one section to the next. They serve the dual purposes of keeping attention focused forward and clarifying logical connections between points. Varied transition tactics include announcing the next point, creating conceptual links between ideas, foreshadowing upcoming topics, and employing transition words like "first," "next," "in contrast," and "consequently." Maintain forward motion by briefly looking ahead to the next point at the end of each section. Avoid mechanically recapping; instead, make points flow together seamlessly. Finally, remove any gaps in the audience's understanding through succinct clarifications of your organizational logic. Crisp, thoughtful transitions keep your speech cohesive, easy to follow, and focused.

Effective Use of Supporting Materials

Vivid supporting materials animate speeches with substance and credibility. Statistics, research, quotations, explanations, anecdotes, examples, and visual aids enrich speeches skillfully. While abundant options are welcome, it also carries the danger of overloading speeches with extraneous information. This section will provide public speaking students with best practices for seamlessly incorporating only the most high-impact supporting materials.

Data and Statistics Spur Audience Interest

Audiences prick up their ears when speakers incorporate numerical data and statistics. Numbers connote factual precision and analytical thinking, immediately commanding attention. Source credible data from reputable organizations, reference survey sample sizes, and cite dates to establish up-to-date relevance. Select data points that demand notice, like surprising comparisons or shocking quantities. Then, translate the meaning of numbers into concrete takeaways for the audience. For example, state that a given statistic means "X would fill this entire room" or "Y equals the population of Chicago." Avoid rubber-stamping speeches with boring lists of numbers or using too many similar statistics. Instead, sprinkle in just enough data at key points to energize your speech with an aura of meticulous research.

Research Adds Scholarly Weight

While data delivers hard numbers, research provides context, explanations, and expert commentary. Audiences grant greater credence and authority when speakers cite qualified research in their speeches. Begin by consulting sources known for rigorous scholarship, like academic journals, think tanks, and government agencies. Briefly summarize notable findings, conclusions, models, or informed opinions supporting your speech points. Always include the study author and publication when first mentioning a study. Beware of citing dated or questionable research from sketchy sources; this can undermine your credibility. Instead, prioritize the most reputable research brands when selecting studies to feature. By referencing respected research appropriately, you reinforce your trustworthiness as a speaker on the topic.

Quotations Add Perspective

Short quotations sprinkled throughout your speech revitalize the tone and grant you the reflected authority of experts or historical figures. When verbally quoting someone, always identify the author first; for famous quotes, just stating the author's name is sufficient. Choose quotes featuring colorfully worded insights from history, literature, science, or popular culture. Keep quotations brief to avoid lacking context or rambling. Before and after the quote, explain its significance: why you selected it and what key takeaways it highlights regarding your speech topic. Avoid overusing too many quotations as a crutch; rely primarily on your original analysis. However, an apt quote at the right moment punches up your authority and memorably crystallizes your point.

Explanations Clarify Complex Concepts

Skilled explainers can illuminate even the most complex subject matters to audiences, especially through analogies, examples, and metaphors. First, break down multifaceted topics into logical steps or parts. Analyze how abstract concepts or processes operate and translate them into concrete terms. Paint verbal pictures of procedures or phenomena using vivid sensory details. Most importantly, compare everyday experiences and objects to activate listeners' existing knowledge. For instance, explain the flow of electricity through wires by likening it to water flowing through pipes. Layering in analogies and examples brings clarity and comprehension even to the most convoluted topics.

Anecdotes Create Emotional Resonance

An anecdote is a short first-person story highlighting a specific event relevant to your speech. Anecdotes establish your credibility through firsthand experience and forge emotional connections with the audience. To incorporate effectively, first set up the context for when the story occurred. Share engaging sensory details that place listeners in the scene with you. Conclude by underscoring the insight about your speech topic or revealing a lesson learned. Avoid meandering or continuing the story too long. The right brief anecdote shared at the perfect moment forges an emotional bond and brings your speech to life.

Examples Illustrate Concepts Vividly

Examples take the clarifying power of explanations one step further by citing or demonstrating specific instances of a principle. Examples range from historical events to current events to personal experiences; the ideal matches your speech purpose and topic. To integrate smoothly, first state the principle, theory, or procedure you want to demonstrate. Briefly describe the salient features of your example. Then, explain how it specifically illustrates the concept, providing vivid details. Wrap up by restating the key lesson the example highlights. Avoid completely irrelevant examples that confuse more than clarify. Vivid examples provide the next best thing to experience firsthand, allowing audiences to grasp concepts through tangible instances instantly.

Visual Aids Clarify and Captivate

Visual aids encompass presentation media like whiteboards, flip charts, physical props, photographs, charts, maps, videos, and slideshows. Visuals serve practical purposes, like clarifying concepts and stirring emotional impact through captivating images and designs. First, align visual choices with your speech purpose; demonstrations work for how-to talks, while graphic images pack a punch for emotional appeals. Then, distill content to concise, bulleted text and bold graphics that enhance your words rather than repeating them. Allow enough time for the audience to fully absorb each visual before continuing. Finally, smoothly incorporate visuals by referring to them at the right moments; avoid flipping back and forth unnecessarily. When used well, visual aids keep attention riveted and make comprehending complex information easy.

Polishing Techniques Transform Good to Great

An otherwise solid speech risks faltering at the last step without vocal polish, careful word choices, and rehearsed delivery. First, incorporate vocal techniques like changing tone, volume, inflection, speed, and pausing for emphasis. Choose vivid words that energize your speech and phrases that rhythmically build to crescendos. Rehearse until your pacing, movements, and transitions feel natural. Polish to eliminate filler words and unnecessary repetition. With practice, powerful delivery will elevate your speech and convey confidence. Avoid reading verbatim or sounding robotic. Remain poised through mistakes. Polishing techniques unite content and delivery into an engaging, smooth-flowing speech.

CHAPTER 4

The Power of Persuasion

While information certainly empowers audiences, inspiration drives them to act upon that knowledge. Master persuasive speakers do more than educate listeners; they motivate them to adopt new beliefs, take action, and effect change. This chapter will unravel the psychology behind persuasive techniques to provide public speaking students with ethical methods for influencing audience attitudes and behaviors.

We will begin by examining core principles of persuasion based on human motivations. You will learn how factors like reciprocity, scarcity, authority, consistency, and liking unconsciously shape our willingness to be persuaded. Next, we will cover common persuasive speaking techniques, including emotional appeals, narrative storytelling, and rhetorical devices. You will gain insight into incorporating techniques ethically and effectively 32, like metaphors, rhyme, contrast, and calls to action, into your speeches.

The heart of this chapter features step-by-step guidance on building rock-solid persuasive arguments. You will learn to make a clear proposition, provide convincing evidence, acknowledge counterarguments, and motivate acceptance through emotional resonance. Following the strategies in this chapter will enable you to construct persuasive speeches and presentations capable of winning over even the most skeptical audiences. Let's get started harnessing the power of ethical persuasion for good!

The Psychology of Persuasion

Attempting to persuade others without first understanding the fundamentals of human psychology is like building a house on a shaky foundation. This section will provide public speaking students with insights from psychology and behavioral economics, revealing how and why people become persuaded. You will gain practical strategies for ethically incorporating core principles of reciprocity, authority, consistency, scarcity, and liking into your persuasive speeches. Knowing how persuasion works psychologically will empower you to craft arguments that resonate deeply with audiences.

Harnessing the Principle of Reciprocity

Humans feel compelled to repay favors, gifts, and concessions others give them. Skilled persuaders utilize this tendency by giving audiences something upfront, like a concession, sample, or compliment. This obligation to reciprocate makes audiences more receptive to the speaker's subsequent requests, whether purchasing a product or embracing an argument. When incorporating reciprocity, first offer the audience a small gift or demonstrate an understanding of their perspective. However, take care to avoid manipulative over-indebtedness. Seek genuine goodwill instead of feeling obligated. With authentic reciprocity established, the audience will repay you with increased openness to your message.

Leveraging the Scarcity Principle

People assign greater value to things that are difficult to obtain or in short supply. Persuaders highlight scarcity by emphasizing limited timeframes, restricted access, high demand, and other constraints. This spikes audience desire and motivates quicker decision-making. Subtly highlight deadlines, eligibility requirements, long waitlists, or capped participation numbers when relevant. However, avoid exaggerating scarcity or lying about availability. Frame scarcity regarding legitimate obstacles listeners face, seizing the opportunity now before them. Scarcity prompts action by capitalizing on our natural aversion to missed chances and limited resources. Use ethically to motivate audiences toward positive goals.

Establishing Yourself as an Authority

Audiences find experts inherently more persuasive than novices. Demonstrating your qualifications, experience, and knowledge on a topic greatly enhances your ability to persuade listeners. Avoid simply stating your credentials; showcase expertise through speech content. Sprinkle in insider details and anecdotes drawn from your work. Quote data and research from studies you conducted or published. Finally, leverage the halo effect of associations with prestigious organizations, educational institutions, and professional certifications affiliated with authority on the topic. Establishing expertise grants instant credibility and influence with audiences inclined to defer to authority figures.

Appealing to the Principle of Consistency

People strive to act consistently with their existing beliefs and values. Persuaders capitalize on this tendency by proving their position aligns with the audience's established viewpoint. Demonstrate a deep understanding of their worldview through language, examples, and values-based reasoning. Seek points of agreement to anchor your premise in their perspective. Avoid direct attacks on sacredly held beliefs; find common ground. With consistency established, audiences will more willingly entertain extending existing positions to align with your well-framed arguments. Consistency crafts pathways to persuade without demanding audiences contradict themselves.

Increasing Liking to Be More Persuasive

We are most easily persuaded by people we know and like. Boost your persuasive appeal by actively building rapport with audiences. Maintain friendly nonverbal signals, pleasant vocal tones, and frequent eye contact. Share upbeat anecdotes highlighting your Humor, humility, and humanity. Compliment the audience and affirm shared hopes and desires. However, avoid crossing into inappropriate familiarity; remain professional. A speaker audibly smiling comes across even on a recording. The more persuasive speakers can make a large audience feel individually liked, the more receptive they will be. However, it must flow from authentic personal charm and respect for listeners.

Avoiding Manipulation and Unethical Persuasion

Equipped with psychological persuasion principles, speakers face the ethical challenge of influencing audiences for good, not ill. Manipulating susceptible people for profit or malice represents an unconscionable abuse of persuasive power. However, ethical persuasion uplifts free thinkers to embrace collectively beneficial change. Promote informed decision-making by clearly presenting a balanced perspective with supporting evidence from reputable sources. Avoid psychological tricks depending on misdirection, confusion, or emotional exploitation. Your influence will face justified backlash if audiences feel manipulated. However, ethically implementing reciprocity, authority, scarcity, consistency, and liking principles creates persuasive speeches capable of changing minds for good.

Persuasive Speaking Techniques

Beyond deep psychological drivers, skilled speakers utilize potent speaking techniques to persuade audiences. This section will explore influential rhetorical devices, including emotional, logical, and credibility-based appeals. You will learn to ethically incorporate rhetorical techniques into your speech, from vivid word pictures to rhyme to strategic repetition. We will also cover compelling storytelling approaches that vividly dramatize your ideas through narrative. Finally, you will gain practical templates and examples for weaving these persuasive techniques into irresistibly convincing arguments. Let us dive into building your skills as an inspiring and masterful persuasive speaker.

Appealing to Emotions Through Pathos

Pathos refers to appealing to the audience's emotions like fear, hope, pride, anger, compassion, and nostalgia to persuade them. Vivid sensory descriptions place listeners directly into emotionally charged scenarios involving people, places, and events. Share moving anecdotes, examples, metaphors, and stories that build empathy and emotional investment. However, avoid overt manipulation like baseless threats, misleading exaggerations, tearjerker ploys, fearmongering, or other unethical tactics. Instead, aim for rational but passionate appeals aligned with your ethical message. With thoughtful pathos established, audiences become receptive to adopting the attitudes, beliefs, and actions you promote.

Establishing Logical Appeals Through Logos

While pathos targets emotions, logos appeals to the audience's logic and reason through statistics, facts, evidence, and explanations. Structure arguments systematically using deductive or inductive reasoning to lead listeners to your desired conclusion. Provide specific evidentiary support from expert testimony, research studies, verifiable statistics, and documented examples. Address potential counterarguments by refuting them logically or pointing out flawed assumptions. Logos convinces audiences by building an intellectual case they can rationally accept. However, avoid overly technical lectures or dry statistical recitations lacking memorable impact. Counterbalance logos with emotionally resonant pathos when presenting persuasive arguments.

Boosting Your Credibility Through Ethos

Ethos references establishing speaker credibility and authority to boost persuasiveness. Demonstrate in-depth knowledge of the topic through your content. Establish common ground though shared values and concerns. Display admirable traits like passion, confidence, likability, and commitment to a cause. Cite years of professional experience, education credentials, awards, prestige associations, publications, and past successes. However, avoid overly lofty claims beyond the scope of your genuine qualifications. While credentials help establish ethos initially, proving your expertise through speech content plays the most critical role. Audiences will embrace your vision more willingly when presented by speakers they respect and trust.

Choosing Rhetorical Devices with Purpose

Adept speakers punctuate speeches with rhetorical devices that embellish ideas linguistically. Alliteration, anaphora, and epistrophe repeat leading consonant sounds, words, or sentence ends for emphasis. Antithesis highlights contrast by juxtaposing opposing ideas in adjacent phrases. Hyperbole offers exaggeration for dramatic effect. Rhetorical questions prompt audience reflection. Triads efficiently present three related messages. Climaxes build verbal crescendos by increasing phrase length and emotional intensity. However, avoid overwhelming speeches with a barrage of unconnected devices. Thoughtfully incorporate select figures of speech at pinnacle moments to crystallize complex ideas into memorable forms. Rhetorical flair helps ideas resonate without overshadowing substance.

Telling Stories for Maximum Persuasive Impact

Audiences perk up their ears at the signal of a story unfolding because our brains are wired to process information through narrative. Stories speak to our shared human experiences. Strategic storytelling in a speech establishes emotional connections with the audience and embodies abstract ideas in concrete reality. Set up the context and major players in your introduction. Build rising action by unfolding events leading to a climax. Conclude with a resolution revealing the core lesson related to your speech topic. Avoid rambling tangents, and clarify how the story specifically illustrated your message. A skillfully told, concise anecdote reaching a poignant ending packs tremendous persuasive power.

Building a Persuasive Argument

We have covered psychological and rhetorical techniques critical for persuasion. Now, let's examine how to construct a complete persuasive argument from start to finish. You will gain a practical step-by-step blueprint for building rock-solid arguments with clear propositions, ample evidence, acknowledgment of alternatives, visually impactful organization, and emotionally resonant conclusions. With these strategies, public speaking students can compose arguments to change entrenched mindsets. Let's begin building compelling cases.

Making a Clear Proposition

Solid arguments begin with a clear, defined proposition or thesis statement asserting your main message or desired action. Avoid fuzzy, rambling ideas. Instead, state succinct propositions clarifying exactly what you advocate: "The city should build a new public library." Propositions explicitly establish your stance while implying that reasonable people could disagree. Make sure to choose propositions that are substantive, debatable, and impactful. A compelling proposition arrests the audience's attention, sparks curiosity, and primes listeners for persuasion with a well-built argument.

Presenting Convincing Evidence

After proposing an argument, the burden of proof falls on you to validate that proposition with logical reasoning and concrete evidence. Provide facts, statistics, examples, and expert testimony demonstrating clear support for your thesis. Quadruple-check sources to ensure data accuracy and relevance. Structure arguments using deductive or inductive logic to build irrefutable cases leading to your conclusion. Address potential counterarguments and present counterevidence to refute them. While emotional resonance supplements intellectual arguments, substantive evidence provides the indispensable foundation of credibility.

Acknowledging Alternate Viewpoints

Persuasion falters by disregarding or ridiculing alternative perspectives. Acknowledge differing viewpoints to build trust and lay the groundwork for common ground. Seek the merits and valid concerns underlying opposing views. Disarm potential objections by legitimizing dissenters' experiences and principles. Understanding core opposing arguments and defining exactly where your proposition differs. Outright rejecting all dissenters as misguided fools will only breed resentment, not open-mindedness. However, the setup lets you emphasize your position's logical and evidentiary strengths. Fair acknowledgment combined with a convincing case best catalyzes changed outlooks.

Structuring Arguments Logically

Organize arguments logically to maximize persuasive impact. Begin by clearly stating your proposition, then lay out primary reasons and supporting evidence. For complex arguments, first, present an overview of key points. Devote sufficient time to elaborate upon each reason or type of evidence. Save your most compelling facts and empathic examples for climactic impact. Structure visuals to showcase patterns of logic and evidence. Finally, summarize key details and restate the proposition as a conclusion. Prioritize logical flow over chronological order. Guide audiences step-by-step toward embracing your proposition. A clear, logical outline provides the indispensable framework for convincing arguments.

Wrapping Up with Emotional Resonance

After systematically building your evidentiary case, supplement its logical appeal with emotional power in your conclusion. Summarize key details and statistics into unifying big ideas and heightened language. Share an inspiring metaphor or famous quote encapsulating your message. Paint a brief word picture envisioning positive change realized. Issue a passionate call to action or collective commitment. However, maintain a truthful, reasonable scope aligned with your evidentiary foundation. Avoid hyperbolic distortions, fearmongering, or far-fetched promises unsupported by your argument. Your concluding flourish should motivate, not manipulate. With substance established, emotional resonance provides the final persuasion push.

CHAPTER 5

Overcoming Social Anxiety

Anxiety represents a significant barrier preventing many people from reaching their public speaking potential. However, psychological research reveals proven techniques to manage anxiety successfully. This chapter will provide public speaking students with strategies to recognize anxious thought patterns and deliberately reframe them. You will gain scientifically backed methods to reduce stress, build self-confidence, and overcome anxiety triggers.

We will begin by identifying common physical, emotional, and cognitive manifestations of social anxiety. Awareness of your anxiety signals and cycles is the first step toward growth. Next, we will explore research-backed techniques to reduce anxiety, including mindfulness practices and systematic desensitization. You will also learn when to seek additional help through counseling or medication.

The bulk of this chapter focuses on reframing anxiety-inducing thoughts through cognitive behavioral therapy techniques. You will gain practical exercises and strategies to dispute distorted anxious thoughts and intentionally replace them with more realistic, empowering mindsets. Our concluding section features advice on configuring small wins to build the self-confidence necessary to confront larger anxiety challenges steadily. Equipped with tools in this chapter, you can break the cycle of avoidance and anxiety to unlock your public speaking gifts. The stage awaits!

Recognizing Social Anxiety Patterns

Social anxiety encompasses excessive fear of embarrassment, judgment, or scrutiny in social situations like public speaking. Physical symptoms of anxiety often trigger fearful thoughts in a cyclical pattern. This section will help public speaking students recognize physical, emotional, and mental manifestations of their social anxiety. Self-awareness of personal anxiety cues and cycles provides the understanding necessary to intervene effectively. Let's shed light on social anxiety's shadowy patterns and power.

Identifying Physical Anxiety Symptoms

Physiological arousal is the body's natural response to perceived threats. However, those with social anxiety experience exaggerated physical reactions even in minimally stressful situations. Learning to identify your physical anxiety symptoms is the first step in managing them. Common symptoms include muscle tension, trembling, sweating, blushing, heart palpitations, dizziness, stomach upset, and hyperventilation. Monitor your body's reactions before and during anxiety-inducing situations like public speaking. Take note of which symptoms manifest most prominently for you. Simply recognizing your typical anxiety physiology provides reassuring clarity and a chance to intervene and calm your body's fearful fight-or-flight response.

Acknowledging Emotional Components

Beyond physical reactions, social anxiety also carries profound emotional consequences, including fear, shame, embarrassment, inadequacy, and lack of confidence. Left unaddressed, these feelings can snowball into depressed mood, isolation, anger issues, and low self-esteem long term. Notice which emotions arise most frequently before, during, and after anxiety-inducing events.

Are fear and embarrassment most prominent for you, or feelings of isolation and depression? Monitoring your emotional state provides insight into both anxiety triggers and downstream impacts. While these feelings can feel intolerable, simply acknowledging them calmly is the first step in mastering them.

Identifying Anxious Thinking Patterns

Cognitive distortions represent exaggerated negative thinking patterns triggering social anxiety. Common distortions include catastrophizing worst-case scenarios, overgeneralizing, selective negative focus, perfectionism, and self-conscious rumination. Which distortions and critical inner voices do you struggle with most? For example, do you meditate over feared outcomes or ruthlessly critique yourself? When facing public speaking, track anxious thoughts racing through your mind. Consider writing down or recording these anxious self-talk scripts to reveal their distorted essence more objectively. Bringing automatic negative thoughts into conscious awareness is immensely powerful for disputing and reframing them.

Recognizing Your Anxiety Cycles

With diligence, you can map how physical, emotional, and mental social anxiety components interconnect for you. Identify your cues a high-anxiety state is building, like muscle tension or self-consciousness. Next, name associated emotional consequences and negative thought patterns likely to follow. Finally, take note of avoidance behaviors or nervous habits like procrastination, overpreparation, drinking, or isolation, which provide temporary relief but reinforce unhealthy anxiety cycles in the long term. While cycles differ among individuals, uncovering your own is illuminating. This self-knowledge is the foundation for breaking anxiety's grip through cognitive, emotional, and behavioral change.

Strategies for Managing Anxiety

Once aware of personal anxiety cycles, public speaking students can deliberately implement strategies to manage anxiety symptoms and triggers. This section will provide techniques to calm the body, mind, and emotions when anxiety strikes. We will cover therapies such as mindfulness, meditation, exposure, and cognitive behavioral approaches backed by psychological research. Medication and professional treatment options will also be discussed. Equipped with tools to short-circuit anxiety cycles, you can reclaim confidence in your communication abilities. Let's delve into techniques to master anxiety.

Using Mindfulness Meditation

Mindfulness meditation training teaches individuals to monitor anxious thoughts and emotions nonjudgmentally without reacting to them. Studies confirm regular mindfulness practice clinically reduces anxiety levels long-term. Set aside 5 to 10 minutes daily to sit quietly, focusing on deep breathing. Observe anxious sensations and thoughts but avoid dwelling on their content. Accept their presence calmly without self-criticism. Imagine fears and emotions slowly dissolving away. Regular mindfulness sessions reduce physiological anxiety responses and negative thought patterns. Before a speech, briefly close your eyes and pay attention to your breath before proceeding mindfully.

Implementing Exposure Therapy

Avoiding feared situations like public speaking reinforces anxiety; facing them systematically combats it through exposure therapy. Start by listing personal anxiety triggers from least to most intimidating. Then, gradually expose yourself to those situations intentionally while practicing remaining calm and mindful. Begin with small steps like a short 1-minute video speech. Slowly work up to longer or live speeches in front of trusted friends, larger groups of acquaintances, and strangers. Avoid retreating from any step until experiencing reduced anxiety. Exposure proves the imagined worst-case never comes true, weakening associated fear. It also builds confidence in abilities to handle challenges through practice.

Exploring Medication and Therapy

For those with severe social anxiety, professional treatment provides additional support. Prescription anti-anxiety medications such as beta blockers help reduce physiological anxiety symptoms for specific stressful events like speeches. However, they carry side effects and do not address root psychological issues long-term. Cognitive behavioral therapy with a licensed counselor equips individuals with healthy coping strategies personalized to their anxiety thought patterns. Group therapy facilitates peer support. Seek professional guidance, especially if anxiety significantly damages the quality of life. Multifaceted approaches combining mindfulness, exposure, and therapy often alleviate social anxiety over time.

Reframing Perfectionistic Mindsets

For some, social anxiety stems from perfectionism and excessive self-criticism. Reframing perfectionistic mindsets that trigger anxiety represents an essential step. Challenging rigid demands and unrealistic standards for yourself opens space for self-compassion. Become aware of inner critics generating unfair critiques. Counter them with realistic assessments of strengths and self-encouragement. Perfection is unattainable and unnecessary; seek constant incremental improvement instead while embracing inevitable mistakes. Remind yourself that good enough is good enough, freeing energy formerly wasted on unreasonable self-judgment. Reframing perfectionism alleviates its accompanying anxiety.

Shifting Nervous Energy into Enthusiasm

Take advantage of the heightened arousal of anxiety by shifting intense nervous energy into passionate enthusiasm instead. Reframe physiological cues like energy, rapid breathing, adrenaline, and restless anticipation as excitement, not dread. Mental energy spent worrying can prepare you if redirected well. Harness feelings productively by thoroughly preparing for speeches and channeling intensity into your voice, gestures, and facial expressions while presenting. Also, use nervous energy to connect with the audience earnestly. Reframing anxiety as eagerness to share your message prevents symptoms from sabotaging your performance. Your body cannot differentiate between nervousness and eagerness - make it work for, not against, you.

Confidence Building Through Small Wins

Lasting confidence emerges gradually by accumulating small wins in anxiety-inducing situations. This section will provide public speaking students with techniques for setting minor achievable goals that build the resilience necessary to overcome intimidating challenges like delivering major speeches. We will cover strategies including celebrating small daily progress, gathering external feedback and validation, and maintaining realistic expectations. With deliberate practice, you can dismantle fear block by block to unveil your inner confident speaker.

Celebrating Daily Progress and Preparation

Major leaps forward start with minor steps. Maintain awareness of and appreciate daily progress toward public speaking goals versus dwelling on perceived inadequacies. Celebrate small wins like two added minutes of practice, slight fear reduction, or moments of authentic audience connection. Track and review improvements to notice your skills steadily compounding over weeks, months, and years. Reflect on how far you've come, not just how far there is to go. Allow the positive momentum of small gains to stretch your comfort zone and deepen self-belief. Daily progress, however gradual, represents the compound interest that builds confidence.

Gathering External Feedback and Validation

Because anxious individuals ignore positive attributes and fixate on flaws, seeking external feedback provides a crucial reality check to build confidence and competence. Ask mentors and trusted peers to critique speeches and presentations.

Collect not just constructive criticism but sincere praise regarding what you do well. Compare your overly critical self-assessments against these external perspectives; a huge gap likely exists. Make notes of every compliment about content, delivery, or rapport with the audience. Review them pre-speech to absorb positive affirmations and counterbalance inner criticism exaggerated by anxiety. Objective praise provides the antidote to perfectionism, validating your skills.

Practicing Realistic Self-Encouragement

Severely anxious speakers benefit from actively coaching themselves with realistic affirmations and constructive advice instead of harsh criticism. Honestly identify 1 or 2 specific skills to improve through the next speech.

Then, actively encourage yourself while practicing and presenting. Silence distorted thoughts like "I'm an awkward failure" with empowering alternatives: "I am improving with each effort. I will inspire people." Address flaws constructively: "Next speech, I'll slow down my speaking pace." Combat fear with rationalizations like "Even if I mess up, it's not catastrophic." Setbacks are inevitable; meet them with self-compassion, not self-blame. Realistic self-encouragement sustains motivation despite anxiety.

Maintaining Perspective on Single Speeches

Whether a success or failure, each speech represents one data point on a lifelong path of public speaking progress. Catastrophizing single performances as defining judgments of abilities causes needless anguish. No speech will be perfect or world-changing.

Rather than judging your entire worth on one outcome, reflect on a speech realistically: "I successfully made key points despite stumbling." Identify areas of learning for future refinement. Then, avoid dwelling to excess on transient past events. Look forward to planning your next opportunity to implement learnings. Neither wallow in failure nor rest on success. No one speech ever wholly defines your skills or future possibilities.

Anchoring Self-Worth Internally

As social anxiety decreases through small wins, you increasingly anchor your sense of self internally rather than basing self-worth on external approval and outcomes. Ask yourself: "Would one harsh critic's opinion negate my value?" Of course not. Your dignity, talents, and humanity remain intact regardless of performance reviews or applause. Self-validation must come from within. As an exercise, write down positive qualities and values defining you beyond any speech. Internalizing your inherent worth builds resilience against anxiety from perceived failure and judgment. You are always intrinsically worthy as a person. Liberate yourself through self-acceptance.

CHAPTER 6

Preparing for Success on Stage

While conceptualizing and writing a presentation provide the content foundation, meticulous preparation and rehearsal transform speeches from mediocre to memorable. This chapter will explore best practices for rehearsing and polishing speeches, dressing for success, and anticipating potential surprises. We will cover techniques to refine timing, pacing, and transitions through practice sessions. You will also learn how to solicit useful observer feedback and incorporate improvements.

Next, we will discuss how strategic dress and grooming choices enhance confidence and audience perceptions. Proper attire boosts credibility for many public speaking contexts and occasions. The chapter concludes by preparing students to handle unexpected situations like technical difficulties, hecklers, or distractions. With extensive rehearsal and adaptable skills, you can exude confidence on opening night, knowing potential curveballs cannot derail your speech's impact. Let's delve into strategies to prepare for public speaking success comprehensively.

Comprehensive Speech Rehearsal

For most, simply reviewing speaking notes constitutes speech "rehearsal." However, transforming a presentation requires exhaustive practice sessions focused on refining pacing, delivery, transitions, and incorporating observer feedback. This section will guide students through essential rehearsal strategies and recommended tweaks to maximize the impact of public addresses. Investing significant rehearsal time elevates adequate speeches into engaging experiences for audiences.

Perfecting Timing and Pacing

Unlike reading at your own pace, public speeches demand adhering to strict timing for overall length and individual sections. Yet dragging, rushing, or inconsistent pacing detracts from audience engagement. Verify total speech length by rehearsing repeatedly from start to finish while monitoring time. Then, adjust section lengths as needed to properly allocate minutes based on importance. If sections consistently exceed or fall short of time targets, rework the content. Next, focus on pacing by evenly spreading words across measured inhales and exhales. Avoid rushing through one breath and then pausing at length before the next. Strive for smooth rhythmic cadence and seamless flow from one phrase to the next. Metronome apps provide helpful pacing guidance.

Practicing Transitions and Segues

Novice speakers often neglect transitions by abruptly jumping between points without direction for the audience. Rehearse, implementing smooth transitions to guide listeners seamlessly between topics. Briefly preview the upcoming point at the end of each section to maintain forward flow. Use transitional phrases like "building upon that," "in contrast," or "similarly" to create conceptual links between ideas. Vary transition language to avoid repetitive mechanical queues. Sharpen segues to elegantly bridge the gap between sections. With practice, transitions become natural extensions of the speech's logical flow. Crisp connections keep attention engaged and prevent listeners from getting lost during scene changes.

Internalizing Content through Repetition

Simply memorizing and reciting a script produces a stiff, robotic delivery lacking authenticity. Instead, use extensive rehearsals to become familiar with material that you internalize content rather than rely on rote memorization. Repeat speeches aloud while continuously refining explanatory language, similes, anecdotes, and descriptions. Let creative enhancements emerge naturally through practice sessions. Gradually break free of transcripts to incorporate more extemporaneous voice and body language. Eventually, speeches should feel like fresh conversations where you fluidly express internalized ideas, not pre-scripted performances. Internalization displays a command of the material, allowing connection with the audience.

Soliciting Feedback from Observers

Even talented speakers need objective observers to identify opportunities for improvement not apparent to the presenter. Recruit a mix of mentors and peers to watch rehearsals and provide candid feedback. Request critiques on pacing, subtle nervous mannerisms, confusing language, visual aid aesthetics, and more. Probe for advice on refining weakest sections. Insist observers feel comfortable offering criticisms, not just praise. Integrate constructive notes into the next practice session. Repeat the feedback process until observers run out of significant improvements. Their outside perspectives provide the mirror necessary for maximal polishing.

Perfecting Vocal Delivery dynamics

Monotone robotic delivery sabotages engagement. Rehearse incorporating intentional variety in volume, tone, speech rate, pronunciation, and inflection. Whisper key phrases for dramatic effect before returning to full voice. Stress critical words louder, higher, or slower. Pause after rhetorical questions or impactful statements. Practice modulating your speaking rate faster and slower. Add expressive emotion congruent with content. However, take care not to overdo dynamics to the point of distraction. Pitch and volume changes should heighten the speech, not draw unnecessary attention. Excellent vocal delivery fully leverages the musical instrument of your voice.

The Role of Dress and Appearance

Many speakers invest heavily in content and delivery practice while neglecting how poor dressing choices can undermine credibility and audience perceptions even before uttering a word. Strategic fashion decisions consciously signal respect for the occasion and listeners through attire. This section will offer students tips on dressing to impress for major public speaking engagements and workplace contexts. Savvy speakers understand clothing's rhetorical power to make positive first impressions and influence listeners.

Dressing Formal for Major Speeches

Certain high-stakes public speaking settings like weddings, graduations, and award ceremonies warrant traditional formal attire aligning with the event's prestige. Gentlemen do well wearing nicely tailored suits with ties and polished dress shoes. Opt for dark or neutral suit colors rather than jarring bright hues. Ladies make lasting elegant impressions in cocktail dresses, pant suits, or dress suits paired with tasteful heels and accessories. Stay away from overly revealing, tight, or risqué clothing. Formal wear demonstrates respect for the venue and the occasion's significance. It signals you took the time to look presentable for this special event.

Business Attire Signals Competence

In corporate, university, or other business contexts, professional business casual or business formal styles project competence and trustworthiness. Gentlemen cannot go wrong matching suits or blazers with button-down shirts and trousers. Ladies impress with blouses, dress pants, or knee-length skirts/dresses paired with flats or low heels. Limit bold patterns or distracting loud jewelry. Avoid sloppy or overly casual jeans, shorts, hoodies, and sneakers. Crisp business attire subtly conveys attention to detail and authority on the topic. However, brands and price tags do not determine worth - polish and taste do.

Casual Presentations Allow More Flexibility

More casual attire creates approachability for informal talks or classroom contexts while still looking put-together. Pair nice jeans or khakis with polos, button-downs, sweaters, or tasteful tees. Ladies can wear a skirt/top combination or casual dresses appropriate for daytime mixed company. Avoid extremes like overly revealing, torn, soiled, or immodest clothing, which detracts rather than adds to distraction. Find the balance between dressing down enough to seem relaxed while demonstrating self-respect. Even casual venues warrant demonstrating you value the audience's time through presentable attire.

Appropriate Grooming and Hygiene

No matter the formality, maintaining hygienic grooming habits always makes powerful first impressions. Arrive with freshly-showered and styled hair. Well-manicured nails and light make-up polish ladies' professional looks. Gentlemen should mind details like clean shaving, trimmed facial hair, and removing lint/pet hair from clothing. Pack breath mints to avoid yawning onion breath. Monitor body odor diligently. While speeches focus on words, failing to exhibit professional grooming and hygiene damages credibility and audience perceptions before you start. Do not underestimate the power of details.

Confidence from Knowing You Look the Part

More than impressing others, strategic speaker attire boosts confidence in your abilities by looking at the credible part. Dressing professionally shows you take the speaking engagement seriously. Fumbling while well-dressed feels less embarrassing than in sloppy attire because you know you prepared your best in all regards. Well-fitting clothing minimizes fidgeting and allows focusing on the message. Pack backup shirts/blouses in case of spills. While clothing does not substitute for content, for most, looking sharp accelerates self-assurance to excel and then presenting. Use clothing to your advantage.

Dealing with Unexpected Challenges

Despite extensive rehearsals and preparation, public speakers must remain adaptable should unexpected challenges arise. This section will equip students with strategies for handling surprises like technical difficulties, distractions, or uncooperative audiences while maintaining composure and professionalism. Preparing contingency plans in advance allows smooth responses during moments of disruption that maintain audience engagement. When the script flips, flexibility and poise set great presenters apart.

Navigating Technical Difficulties

Despite meticulous preparation, technology often fails at inopportune moments during speeches. Projection screens go blank, mics cut out, videos freeze, or PowerPoints crash unexpectedly. Pause and troubleshoot quickly but avoid dwelling excessively on problems and derailing your speech's flow. Have backups like printouts or remote slide advancers ready as contingencies. If issues persist, proceed to speak without visual aids until resolved later. Avoid flustered reactions or comments that amplify frustration. Handle mishaps breezily, then quickly refocus the audience's attention on your confident delivery and captivating content.

Managing Uncooperative Audience Members

Rude audiences can also derail speeches if caught off guard. Hecklers interject irrelevant questions to challenge speakers. Rowdy spectators talk loudly among themselves despite requests for attention. Phones audibly ring as owners take calls mid-speech. First, defuse tense situations with Humor, if appropriate. Respectfully refuse tangential questions by redirecting focus. Do not engage hecklers directly. If polite interventions fail, calmly call out unacceptable behavior with non-aggressive language. Alert event organizers to repeat disruptions involving certain individuals if necessary. Refuse to let inconsiderate actions sabotage your composure or concentration.

Staying Poised through External Distractions

Occasionally, environmental circumstances outside your control threaten to disrupt speech concentration. Noisy construction, sirens, or announcements may drown out words. Power outages or extreme weather pose unexpected challenges. Longwinded award recipients leave you no time. View such inconveniences as opportunities to display grace under pressure. Pause briefly, then repeat critical content if outside noise interrupts you. Adjust the speaking volume if listeners indicate difficulty hearing. If power goes out, amplify your voice and proceed unplugged; let your confidence shine. Demonstrating flexibility amidst suboptimal circumstances earns the audience respect.

Recovering Smoothly from Mistakes

Despite endless rehearsals, everyone occasionally flubs during live speeches through mispronunciations, forgetting words, or mixing up sequences. Do not call excessive attention to errors through awkward apologies or self-deprecating jokes. Quickly correct mispronounced terms and move forward as if the mistakes never occurred. If you truly draw a blank, pause naturally as if for effect before immediately continuing your point. Omit forgotten sections if unable to recover the thought trail quickly. Persevere without breaking composure, dwelling awkwardly, or criticizing yourself mid-speech. Audiences respect poise despite imperfections far more than anxious reactions.

Practicing Impromptu Speaking

The best method for building adaptability is training through impromptu speech exercises. Rehearse spontaneously, expounding on surprise topics with no preparation. Mindfully turn nervousness into excitement for the challenge. Begin with 1-minute mini-speeches between friends to grow comfortable thinking extemporaneously. Gradually increase impromptu lengths and difficulty. Eventually, incorporate unplanned speeches into professional presentations. Impromptu experience boosts quick thinking and recovery skills to manage real surprises adeptly. With practice, engaging content weaves itself when you relinquish rigid control. Learn to welcome unpredictability.

CHAPTER 7

Delivering Impactful Speeches

While speech content provides the core foundation, delivery often determines success in connecting with audiences. Masterful speakers utilize strategic vocal techniques, nonverbal body language, and audience engagement to convey ideas memorably. This chapter will equip public speaking students with research-backed skills to confidently deliver speeches in a polished, charismatic style.

We will begin by exploring critical nonverbal dimensions, including posture, hand gestures, facial expressions, and eye contact. You will learn to project confidence through open stances and avoid distracting mannerisms. Next, we will cover proven vocal techniques to dynamically modulate volume, tone, rate of speech, and inflection. Speeches come alive when voice aligns with content.

Finally, the chapter will detail interactive strategies to engage audiences through Humor, emotion, questions, and participation. Speeches transform into two-way conversations when listeners feel immersed as participants. This chapter will empower public speakers to make lasting impacts on audiences by combining content mastery with research-based delivery techniques. Let's bring your speeches to life!

Nonverbal Communication

Standing stationary behind podiums stifles engagement. Skilled speakers strategically leverage nonverbal behavior to complement words. This section will guide public-speaking students on using body language, hand gestures, facial expressions, and eye contact to deliver speeches dynamically. Research shows audiences rely more heavily on speakers' nonverbal cues than verbal content. Mastering nonverbal delivery is critical for bringing messages to life.

Using Effective Body Language

Audiences subconsciously ascertain competence, confidence, and rapport from speakers' posture, stance, and proximity. Project credibility by standing tall with open shoulders. Avoid rounded slouching or crossed arms reading as closed off. Claim your physical space on stage through free movement and expansive gestures without clinging to notes or podiums for comfort. Pause purposefully at the front edge of stages for direct audience connection versus hiding behind furnishings. Appropriate pacing immerses listeners in your flow versus bouncing anxiously. Your physicality frames how audiences receive content.

Incorporating Strategic Hand Gestures

Thoughtfully incorporated hand gestures and movements add essential visual interest and reinforce speech concepts. However, unrestrained waving quickly becomes distracting. Time gestures strategically to accentuate key points, descriptions, contrasts, and sequences. Paint pictures in the air through illustrative movements, conjuring concrete images complementing your words. Lower volume briefly when extending arms for emphasis so gestures do not compete with vocals for attention. Avoid distracting mannerisms like jingling coins in pockets, pen clicking, or fidgeting hands by keeping them purposefully engaged in strategic motions. Let gestures pull listeners deeper into your speech.

Showcasing Expressive Facial Animation

Facial expressions displaying genuine passion and emotion widen audience engagement and recall far more effectively than monotone monologues. But exaggerating for effect risks undermining sincerity if overdone. Apply the golden rule: demonstrate positive enthusiasm and reactions you would appreciate as an audience member yourself. Smile naturally when sharing humorous anecdotes, inspiring visions, or heartfelt appreciation.

Convey somber sentiments through furrowed brows but avoid grimacing. Rehearse in mirrors until facial movements feel authentic, not performative. Vivid expressions, like gestures, provide the flash needed to ignite speeches into animated experiences.

Making Direct Eye Contact

Frequent intentional eye contact embodies the singular fastest route to forging audience connection. However, continually staring or avoiding eye contact entirely sabotages rapport. Master natural patterns by regularly cycling gaze evenly across all listeners. Pause a few seconds on each face to personalize engagement before moving on. Briefly avert your focus when needing to gather thoughts before returning attention outward. Avoid reading off notes or slides without looking up. When conversing feels overwhelming, focus on foreheads instead of direct eye contact. Practice sustaining eye contact through speeches to keep listeners feeling seen.

Vocal Techniques

Beyond nonverbals, confident, flexible voices captivate and persuade. This section details research-based vocal techniques to make speeches more dynamic, articulate, and engaging. You will learn specific skills for modulating volume, tone, rate of speech, and inflection appropriately during presentations. Voice training lifts language off pages into experiences listeners viscerally feel through adept auditory delivery.

Modulating Volume Effectively

Speak loudly enough for those in the back to hear clearly without straining while avoiding screaming or monotone mumbling. Adjust volume purposefully rather than staying static. Increase loudness to highlight passionate crescendos or critical information. Lower briefly for tension before returning louder. Practice altering projection based on room size and amplification. Take advantage of microphones for large venues by focusing on clear enunciation versus shouting unnaturally. Record rehearsals and adjust levels until reaching optimal decibels. Purposeful volume modulation smooths natural rhythms.

Varying Tone Appropriately

Adapting tone color illustrates contrasts, underscores emotions, and reveals inner states. Deepen tone briefly to emphasize serious content before gently raising back up. Sharpen a usually soft-spoken tone to accentuate urgency on key points. Let your voice reflect the feelings and meanings you aim to convey. However, take care not to overdramatize unnaturally. Avoid extensively straining vocal cords by forcing pitch beyond comfortable range. Monitor recordings to ensure tonal quality remains clear and pleasant despite new variations. With practice, the tone becomes a subtle paintbrush for shading speeches.

Managing Speech Pace Strategically

Pace refers to your rate of speech delivery measured in words per minute. Speaking too slowly or quickly hampers processing and engagement. Find an upbeat cadence slightly above normal conversational pace. Accelerate and slow strategically rather than remaining monotonous. Quicken to express excitement but slow for solemnity or to stress pivotal concepts. Take care not to race ahead of listeners' ability to absorb information. Insert intentional dramatic pauses to let key points resonate before continuing. Clean up filler words cluttering pace. Listeners will invest more focus in decoding your messages if you meet them at an optimal pace.

Using Inflection for Vocal Dynamism

Inflection refers to changing vocal pitch within sentences. Too much monotonous vocal fry bores ears. But excessive sing-songy fluctuations sound unnatural. Practice emphasizing keywords and varying cadence mid-sentence to maintain interest. Stress unexpected words in a series to highlight contrasts. Lift your voice at the end of rhetorical questions. Descend for declarative points but ascend for open-ended uncertainty. Record and analyze speeches to ensure you avoid repetitive inflection patterns. With rehearsal, infusing your voice with energy through varied emphasis comes naturally.

Audience Engagement Strategies

Beyond polish and presence, great speeches actively involve audiences through Humor, emotion, asking questions, and participation. This section will equip public speakers with specific techniques to engage listeners as dynamic participants. Speaking "at" passive audiences presents lectures. Speaking "with" audiences creates shared experiences and forges human connections. Let's explore skills for making speeches collaborative, not one-sided.

Appropriately Using Humor

Audiences instantly warm to speakers with genuine Humor woven smoothly into speeches through anecdotes, jokes, and amusement at life's quirks. However, forced Humor bombs are painful. Carefully select 1-2 humorous stories or clean jokes relevant to your topic and audience. Pause briefly for laughter to dissipate before continuing content. Smile good-naturedly at the amused reactions you provoke without going overboard seeking laughter. Weave in observations of shared funny frustrations. Humor relieves stress and makes difficult topics approachable. But avoid unprofessional stand-up routines or distracting antics undermining content. Laughter opens hearts and minds.

Harnessing the Power of Emotion

Stirring emotions like inspiration, nostalgia, or curiosity bonds speakers and audiences in the shared experience. However, overt manipulation feels disingenuous. Identify 1-2 moments in speeches that are naturally ripe for emotional impact. For instance, pay heartfelt tribute to honor recognizable heroes. Share brief, poignant personal anecdotes about your content that forged your perspective. Avoid sentimentality, but speak stirringly from the heart regarding values motivating you. Circulate beforehand to learn audience concerns to address thoughtfully. With authenticity, emotional resonance uplifts even ordinary occasions into meaningful experiences.

Asking Questions to Create Dialogue

Transform speeches from passive monologues into active dialogues by frequently asking audiences rhetorical and direct questions. Simple poles like "Raise your hand if you've experienced this." provide quick intimacy. Ask thoughtful questions and allow time for inner reflection before continuing. Offer new perspectives for consideration. Brainstorm engaging prompts specific to your talk, like "When was the first time you noticed this issue?" Questions invite audiences into the co-creation of meaning versus imparting wisdom one-directionally. Discussions foster deeper learning and connection than lectures.

Incorporating Audience Participation

Even more, interaction arises when audiences verbally or physically participate in speeches. Invite volunteers on stage for simple demonstrations. Pass out worksheets for groups to complete quick activities or discuss prompts. Assign friendly competition games between sections. Provide paper for brief written responses you collect and incorporate. Polls and show of hands keep everyone involved simultaneously. However, notify organizers beforehand if planning major interactive components. Facilitate segments crisply without losing control. Active participation makes messages memorable through direct experiential learning.

Managing Q&A Sessions Effectively

Expect presenting without fielding questions rarely. Master Q&A by repeating questions aloud first to clarify and buy thinking time. Address the audience generally, not just questioners. If you don't immediately know the answers, buy time by thanking askers and promising to follow up later. Consolidate multiple questions into one concise response when able. Avoid wasting time on irrelevant or hostile questions; tactfully refocus on central topics. Take control as moderator to spread questions evenly over all segments. Project confidence through vocal tone and body language regardless of surprise inquiries. Handled well, Q&A reinforces expertise and provides memorable wrap-ups.

CHAPTER 8

Handling Q&A and Feedback

Speeches rarely conclude without contending with audience questions or critiques. Navigating post-presentation Q&A sessions and feedback demonstrates communication mastery equal to the initial performance. This chapter will equip public speaking students to conclude presentations strongly through strategies for facilitating insightful Q&A, embracing constructive feedback, and continuously improving skills.

We will begin by outlining techniques to manage Q&A productively. You will learn tactics from reiterating questions to strategically calling on audience members. We will also cover smoothly handling difficult inquiries and transitions into wrap-ups. Next, the chapter explores receiving feedback with maturity from observers, mentors, and peers to implement improvements.

Finally, we will examine developing self-awareness to continually refine your speaking skills through video review, metrics analysis, and mindful self-critique. The same presentation is never truly finished. Consistently honing your craft through feedback and reflection separates good from masterful speakers. Let's discover skills for sticking to the landing of public speaking engagements.

Strategies for Successful Q&A Sessions

Most speeches culminate with an audience Q&A session before closing. Fielding questions represents a critical final opportunity to address confusion, showcase expertise, and strengthen audience connection. However, uncontrolled Q&A often rambles aimlessly.

This section will equip public speaking students to facilitate organized Q&A interactions that reinforce speech ideas and speaker credibility. Let's explore how to stick Q&A landings.

Repeat and Clarify Each Question

After a question is asked, resist launching into immediate answers. First, repeat the question aloud or paraphrase it to verify understanding from the asker. Rephrasing also reiterates the initial inquiry for the wider audience's benefit before answering. Take advantage of repeating questions to gather your thoughts and frame helpful responses.

Ask the original questioner to confirm you captured the essence of their query before proceeding. Iterating questions promotes thoughtful exchange and keeps everyone in the loop.

Address the Entire Audience

Answer questions to the room generally rather than engaging single questioners in exclusive side conversations. Connect your gaze with various audience sections to draw everyone into your response explanations. Begin replies with lead-ins like "As the question highlights..." to incorporate the entire audience into dialogue. Discussing questions communally avoids isolating exchanges and enables all to feel involved in conclusions. For large events, stand centrally on stage when managing Q&As to symbolize addressing the collective audience.

Manage Time and Questioner Selection

Pre-allocate total Q&A time limits and individual question durations to avoid open-ended meandering. Cue questioners before their turn, saying, "In the front row next." Gently interrupt rambling questions by validating briefly, then redirecting focus. Prevent any one person from monopolizing the exchange. Call on different audience sections purposefully to prevent a few loud voices from dominating. If needed, inquire, "Are there any first-time questioners who have not had a chance yet?" Time limits maintain structure while allowing broad participation.

Strategic Call Order to Break the Ice

Consider your first questioner carefully to set the tone. Lead with supporters first to build momentum before potentially critical individuals. Start with easy warm-up questions before complex or challenging ones. Identify subject experts spread throughout the audience.

Call on them to indirectly reinforce your credibility when they validate your content depth through pleased reactions or follow-up congruence. Carefully orchestrating question order prevents early negativity from derailing exchanges while providing examples of ideal interactions.

Address Challenging Questions Tactfully

Inevitably, some questions attempt to attack speakers' credibility, go off-topic, or create distractions. First, calmly repeat the challenging question to the group. Respond graciously by identifying valid points before refocusing strategically. For example: "You raise a fair concern regarding X.

However, to bring this back to the main topic..." Defuse heated questions through non-defensive empathy. Manage inappropriate outbursts by immediately redirecting attention: "Let's please stay focused on our central theme of..." Do not take the bait and remain unflappable.

Wrap Up with Impactful Reflections

Leave the audience powerfully impacted by dedicating the last 5-10 minutes to unstructured reflections beyond questions. Synthesize key themes, inspirational takeaways, and future directions.

Offer bold perspectives for further consideration. Unscripted wrapping thoughts represent your unique closing gift before parting ways. Stand center stage, making eye contact to recreate intimacy as you begin your speech. Seal presentations with wisdom resonating long after the applause subsides.

Constructive Feedback Reception

Beyond Q&A in real-time, mastering subsequent feedback demonstrates the hallmark of exceptional public speakers. This section will guide students on proactively soliciting observer critiques and humbly embracing criticism. Feedback provides the mirror necessary for self-improvement by highlighting developmental opportunities not apparent from the speaker's limited onstage perspective. Let's cultivate maturity by accepting imperfect performances and utilizing feedback for growth.

Seeking Constructive Critique

Superb speakers actively invite detailed, constructive feedback from trusted advisors after speeches rather than passively awaiting compliments or complaints. Specifically, request critical reactions focused on two aspects done well and two needing improvement. Ask observers to detail which components detracted from engagement or confused understanding. Prompt advisors to recommend concrete techniques that could enhance future speeches. Silently take notes without defensiveness. Soliciting critical feedback displays a commitment to maximizing public speaking impact through ongoing refinement.

Acknowledging Valid Criticism

When receiving negative feedback, immediately thank advisors for their honesty and begin identifying valid points thoughtfully. Digest constructive critiques before responding emotionally or dismissing criticisms prematurely. Ask observers to expand upon concerns to understand their perspective fully. Express humility at opportunities for improvement listeners reveal from their vantage points. Valid critiques give gifts enabling your growth should you choose to receive them that way. All great speakers still have progress yet to make.

Clarifying Vague Feedback

If initial feedback seems excessively vague, like "work on delivery," tactfully request specific elaboration. For example, say, "Thank you. Can you explain more about aspects of delivery I can improve?" Vague feedback often stems from advisors hesitating to share critical reactions. Warmly reassuring your openness to specifics empowers details to emerge. Drill into vague generalities until you uncover actionable advice on what skills to build. Listen intently to glean every nuance for translating into positive change.

Implementing Feedback Incrementally

Resist completely overhauling your presentation style overnight in response to feedback. Radical contradictory changes only confuse audiences expecting your brand. Instead, isolate 1-2 pieces of advice most aligned with your strengths to begin implementing immediately at your next speech. For example, start speaking 5% slower if critiqued for racing pace. Film yourself presenting again afterward to assess incremental improvements, then gradually incorporate more suggestions. Sustainable growth results from orderly small enhancements integrated coherently over successive speeches, not overnight in the 180s.

Monitoring Emotional Reactions

Candid feedback often provokes emotional knee-jerk reactions, especially if you feel insecure speaking publicly. Notice defensiveness, anger, or excuses arising internally and acknowledge these emotions mindfully without reacting automatically. If needed, delay providing any defensive verbal reactions at the moment. Process feelings afterward alone through journaling. Then, revisit feedback objectively once raw emotions have settled. Thank advisors again the next day for caring enough to help you grow. Managing emotional reactions requires maturity but enables accurately identifying truths in critiques.

Continuous Improvement through Self-Reflection

Beyond observer feedback, exceptional public speakers constantly self-monitor speeches through video review, output metrics, and mindful self-critique to continuously elevate skills. This section will provide students with techniques for pinpointing their developmental opportunities and incrementally refining them through consistent self-reflection. Let's explore building the self-awareness and work ethic necessary for ongoing mastery.

Video Recording for Objective Review

Review recordings of speeches to notice improvement opportunities beyond what on-site observers catch related to nervous tics, ineffective pacing, stiffness, and more. Film from auditorium perspectives to simulate external audience experiences versus your stage vantage point. Watch recordings multiple times to absorb nuances. Take copious notes on distracting mannerisms, confusing language, and pacing lulls. Strive to detach emotionally when self-critiquing. Share videos with mentors for additional feedback. Frequent video review provides indispensable concrete awareness.

Tracking Performance Metrics

Quantify speaking success metrics like audience size, applause duration, audible reactions, question quantity, and survey ratings over successive speeches. Graph trends to visualize patterns in speaking aptitude. Take notes on why certain metrics improved or declined. Strive to incrementally better key indicators through practice and refinement. However, avoid relying only on superficial quantitative marks that fail to capture speech essence. Balance metrics with qualitative advisor feedback for complete awareness. Measurements make improvement tangible.

Reflecting on Mindset Shifts Needed

Beyond technical skills, reflect on mental and emotional mindset adjustments that could elevate your speaking prowess. Do confidence issues plague you? Is self-consciousness inhibiting natural delivery? Are perfectionistic expectations causing excessive anxiety? Does fear of criticism restrict risk-taking? Journal deeply on inner outlooks requiring development and possible baby-step solutions. For example, incrementally practice speeches in front of supportive friends first if anxiety overwhelms larger crowds. Mindset breakthroughs unlock greater behavior improvements.

Targeting Specific Skills for Focused Growth

Beyond generally improving, isolate 2-3 specific presentation skills to develop intensively during the next few speeches. For example, focus solely on implementing more dramatic pregnant pauses for emphasis. Track incremental progress in mastering defined abilities through repetition at each subsequent talk. Avoid tackling too many new skills simultaneously. Mastery requires concentrated effort on a few capabilities at a time. Target priority development areas until excelling before moving on. Consistent incremental skill sharpening compounds over the years into expertise.

Celebrating Small Improvements through Journaling

Documenting progress provides an encouraging perspective during long Plateaus of public speaking improvement. Maintain a journal cataloging micro-wins like slightly increased eye contact duration, better vocal projection, or a joke successfully landing. Review past journal entries periodically to remind yourself of how far you have developed while keeping focus forward on the next achievable baby step. Celebrate any microscopic gains through journaling to sustain motivation during difficult mastery journeys requiring years. You are farther along than you imagine.

CHAPTER 9

The Impact of Technology on Public Speaking

Technology's meteoric evolution constantly shapes and expands modern public speaking opportunities while introducing new challenges. This chapter will equip readers to leverage digital presentation tools and virtual speaking formats effectively for maximum impact.

We will explore best practices for slide deck creation, video integration, speech recording, and broadcasting to online audiences. You will gain strategies for translating in-person skills into virtual presented environments. While in-person gatherings remain irreplaceable, supplemental technological capabilities now allow public speakers to reach and inspire at scales unimaginable just decades ago. Let's delve into public speaking skills for the digital age!

Leveraging Presentation Software

Mastering presentation software enables impactfully integrating visuals to complement speeches before live or virtual audiences. This section will guide public speakers on skillfully creating slide decks with PowerPoint and other tools that captivate visually without distracting or overwhelming. You will gain tips from designing aesthetically pleasing templates to seamlessly weaving in multimedia while avoiding common pitfalls like "death by PowerPoint." Thoughtful creation and careful presentation timing can elevate slides from forgettable to integral presentation element audiences eagerly anticipate.

Designing Visually Appealing Slide Templates

Even before inputting content, thoughtfully conceive slide deck templates aligning with your brand and speech purpose that capture attention as soon as they appear. Select 1-2 complementary fonts and consistent formatting for text across all slides.

Add tasteful logos, color schemes, backgrounds, and spacing aligned with your or your organization's style guide. Choose ample empty space around text instead of cramming pages. Confirm all visual elements render clearly on both projectors and mobile screens. Aesthetic slide template design demonstrates your professionalism while creating instant audience goodwill.

Utilizing High-Quality Photos and Graphics

When selecting visuals, prioritize simple high-resolution photography and graphics over complex clipart or distracting animation. Choose pictures and icons reinforcing key points metaphorically through clear symbolism appreciable at a glance.

Never stretch low-quality images pixilated on screen. Check that backgrounds clearly contrast the text. Include attribution citations for all imagery. One vivid picture can encapsulate an entire speech point through visual storytelling. However, avoid slideshows deteriorating into irrelevant picture galleries lacking continuity. Each visual should connect explicitly to topics.

Modulating Text and Formatting Strategically

While compelling visuals catch attention, strategic text inclusion provides the necessary substance. Summarize key data, statistics, or quotes central to each point in concise bullet points, not dense paragraphs. Limit bullets to 6 words at most. Chunk long lists under subheadings for scannability. Vary bullet font sizes and colors to emphasize hierarchy.

Avoid text walls that quickly lose audiences. Implement accessible options like increased font sizes and color contrast modes for vision-impaired viewers. When formatted engagingly, sparing text provides helpful structural reinforcement, making comprehension smooth.

Seamlessly Incorporating Videos and Motion Graphics

Audiovisual media like short videos, animated graphics, and audio narration clips diversify presentations with multimedia engagement. However, excessive multimedia risks cognitive overload and technical difficulties. Choose 1-2 videos under 2 minutes framed by context explaining their relevance. Select motion graphics purposefully to demonstrate processes or concepts that are difficult to convey verbally.

Preview all clips to guarantee school/workplace appropriateness and remove insensitive content. Embed media cleanly with seamless transitions on either side, whether silly or serious, strategic audiovisual integration allows the conveying of messages and emotions beyond just spoken words.

Practicing Smooth Presenter-Slide Interplay

Far beyond merely presenting slides, masterfully incorporate decks as visual guides synchronizing with speech content flow. Rehearse slide change timing until you know sequences intuitively.

Preview upcoming slides using transitional phrases like "As this next slide illustrates..." to maintain flow. Avoid reading straight from slides but use images to reinforce points through natural gestures. Pause at key moments for audiences to fully digest slide information before continuing. Perfectly timed delivery elevates slides from passive backdrop to active synchronized enrichment.

Avoiding Communication Pitfalls

With PowerPoint's powers come potential perils of distracting design choices and information overload sabotaging communication. Avoid dense, unreadable text, garish animations, and overwhelming slide counts exceeding 1 per minute.

These elements overstimulate visual channels, causing audiences to exhaustively process slides rather than listening to your speech. Prioritize clean aesthetics, strategic text, and thoughtful multimedia incorporation. Demonstrate mastery by intentionally limiting slides to highlight only the most essential supporting elements. Less is more when allowing your compelling speech itself to shine.

Virtual Public Speaking Tips and Techniques

Public speaking in online virtual settings like webinars, teleconferences, or prerecorded videos continues expanding in the digital age. This section will provide tips to translate in-person public speaking skills seamlessly into effective virtual delivery equally capable of informing and inspiring audiences.

You will gain strategies for building rapport through cameras, speaking dynamically without in-person reactions, and utilizing digital presentation tools for engagement. With deliberate practice, virtual speeches can achieve similar human connection and impact.

Building Rapport and Intimacy Remotely

Unlike live events, virtual speeches contend with audiences potentially multitasking instead of offering full attention. Counteract distraction by purposefully building personal rapport even through screens.

Frequently make gentle eye contact directly into the camera to approximate the in-person connection. Share fun personal anecdotes and amused reactions to foster a sense of relationship. Display warmth and passion using vocal inflections and facial expressions captured on video. Ask questions and defer to viewer comments in chat channels. Virtual intimacy inspires the same levels of trust in speakers' knowledge and goodwill.

Gesturing Naturally without In-Person Cues

Gesturing naturally feels less comfortable without live audience visual feedback. Avoid unnatural, exaggerated gesticulation. Instead, envision a supportive friend while speaking and gesturing to them.

Use hand motions to shape ideas rather than forcefully trying to stir reactions. Practice before recordings with timers to build physical presence skills that are transferable live later. Mute videos afterward to assess whether gestures visually support verbal content without sound as a crutch. Thoughtfully incorporated natural movement boosts nonverbal connection even from screens.

Speaking Dynamically to Sustain Energy

When speaking virtually, presenters' energies can deflate without live audience reciprocal reactions. Counteract flat delivery by intentionally varying rate, volume, tone, and inflection. View analytics to assess whether attention drops during slower sections. Speed up delivery slightly or throw in humor to reengage participants.

Listen to recordings and adjust any monotonous sections. Training before mirrors builds lively expression without requiring ongoing reactions. Remember viewers' limited attention spans and intentionally work to actively sustain dynamic vocal momentum.

Utilizing Digital Tools to Engage Viewers

Abundant digital presentation tools foster creative audience engagement in virtual speeches. Display visually engaging slides highlighting key ideas. Splice in short comedic video clips. Use annotation tools to circle or underline central points on desktop shares.

Embed opinion polls or comprehension quizzes. If presenting live, pause for responses to chat questions. Follow-up recordings with supplemental resources in email summaries. Take advantage of presentation software features to avoid static delivery. The more you creatively leverage tools only available virtually, the more dynamic your speeches become.

Leveraging Asynchronous Videos Strategically

Prerecording video speeches offers flexibility at the cost of losing real-time audience interaction. Boost replay value by interspersing brief, engaging commentary addressing future viewers: "As you'll see here..." Include B-roll footage from multiple angles like closeups for visual variety.

Create quick on-screen graphics highlighting key statistics or terms mentioned. Provide downloadable resources in video descriptions to apply lessons. Finally, keep asynchronous videos concise at 5-15 minutes maximum to respect limited viewer attention spans. Well-produced tight videos deliver memorable speeches audiences will enthusiastically rewatch.

Online Platforms for Speaking Practice and Broadcast

Technology provides revolutionary new platforms to both practice speeches and reach global audiences at scale. This section explores modern websites, apps, and channels allowing convenient public speaking development.

You will also gain insights into strategically broadcasting presentation recordings to expand your impact and visibility as a thought leader. Let's investigate techniques for leveraging technology to grow from novice to expert speaker while spreading messages worldwide.

Toastmasters for Friendly Skill Development

For affordable practice in front of live audiences, join a local Toastmasters International club. Members work through structured speech programs among supportive fellow learners. In-person meetings help overcome live delivery fears. Members also provide helpful feedback. However, options exist to join virtual clubs using video conferencing technologies if geographic clubs are unavailable. The path to excellence starts by taking advantage of Toastmasters for low-pressure development opportunities in accessible local settings. Consistent practice and incremental growth achieve dramatic long-term results.

Additional Apps and Communities for Practice

Beyond Toastmasters, apps like Podium and Oratr allow uploading practice speech videos for virtual feedback and critiques from coaches worldwide. Massive open online courses (MOOCs) on public speaking provide structured lesson plans. Joining online communities like r/publicspeaking on Reddit enables asking fellow learners questions.

Practicing speeches on video call apps like Zoom builds technical fluency. Evaluate the pros and cons of various modern platforms and services to customize an optimal technology toolkit supplementing your learning. Abundant digital options exist to hone skills.

Building a Public Speaking Portfolio

As skills progress, develop an online portfolio showcasing speech excerpts and credentials to establish credibility as an expert speaker. Collect representative video highlights demonstrating key abilities like audience interaction, humor, and poise under pressure.

Compile presentation slide decks illustrating planning capabilities. List speaking awards, education credentials, and noteworthy venues. Portfolios validate expertise and thought leadership, helping secure higher-profile engagements. They also build professional development by documenting growth over successive years. Treat portfolios as living documents expanded throughout your public speaking journey.

Optimizing and Sharing Presentation Recordings

Recording speeches provides valuable replay material for self-assessment, future marketing, and sharing with wider audiences, which was rarely possible before the digital age. Obtain consent first before publication and retention when presenting.

Ensure quality audio and video capture using multimedia equipment. Trim recordings to key segments before posting on YouTube, social media, or personal websites. Write detailed descriptions summarizing core topics, insights, and timestamps. Share engaging excerpts to give audiences a preview taste, spurring interest in your thought leadership. Take advantage of recording speeches as an opportunity for exponential impact.

Leveraging Mass Distribution Platforms Ethically

Modern digital channels like viral social media and mass emails enable potentially reaching millions of viewers on an unprecedented scale. However, avoid aggressively manipulating or misleading audiences solely to drive views and followers. Frame messages and appeals truthfully. Honor consent preferences regarding data privacy and email subscriptions. Seek primarily to create value by educating, inspiring, or empowering audiences ethically. Measure success not by superficial viral shares but by meaningful human connections. Responsible use of technological reach poses a profound opportunity to spread uplifting ideas worldwide.

CHAPTER 10
Public Speaking Ethics

While public attention focuses on polished delivery, ethical foundations represent the indispensable bedrock upholding successful communications. This chapter will guide readers through core areas of public speaking ethics, including properly attributing sources, respecting diverse groups, and avoiding manipulative persuasion. You will gain practical strategies for elevating both the authenticity and morality of your public messages.

We will begin by exploring principles and citation formats to fully credit research, statistics, stories, and multimedia originating from outside sources. Next, the chapter will cover sensitivity tactics for inclusive messaging, embracing varied demographics and perspectives. Finally, we will examine ethical persuasion techniques focused on rational empowerment rather than manipulation.

Following ethical best practices earns audiences' respect and trust while establishing speakers as sources of integrity. Public speeches wield immense influence. This chapter will equip readers to consciously wield that power to uplift others ethically through words. Let us explore the critical foundations upholding your honorable voice.

Plagiarism and Citing Sources

Ethical public speaking begins with ensuring full, accurate attribution of any ideas, facts, or multimedia originating from identifiable outside sources. Plagiarism erodes a speaker's credibility and betrays audiences' trust. This section will guide readers in properly crediting research, avoiding plagiarism, and implementing citation best practices as outlined by style guides. Establishing meticulous attribution habits upholds the dignity of your voice against any doubt.

Defining and Avoiding Plagiarism

Plagiarism involves utilizing any content created by others while failing to properly acknowledge its source. This encompasses outright stealing full written passages but also uncredited paraphrasing of source ideas in your own words. Even inadvertent neglecting of citations constitutes academically dishonest plagiarism. To avoid this, comprehensively cite sources consulted during speech preparation using the recommended formatting explained in the following subsections. If unsure, err on the side of over-attributing sources to demonstrate commitment to transparency. Audiences will respect diligent acknowledgment of sources elevating your content.

Crediting Written Research Sources

For written publications like books, journal articles, or website pages used as sources, include in-text parenthetical citations noting the author and year of publication. For example, mention a study's findings, then follow with (Smith, 2022) denoting author and year within parentheses. More detailed references should then appear under a formatted bibliography or works cited list at the speech conclusion. Adhere precisely to style guide rules on constructing citations and reference lists from formats like APA, MLA, or Chicago. Consult guides for proper syntax citing multiple authors, group organizational authors, or lacking publication years or authorship.

Acknowledging Multimedia Sources

Public speakers frequently utilize supporting multimedia like videos, graphs, images, infographics, or audio clips embedded within presentations. Before including supplementary multimedia, diligently verify copyright permissions or utilize only public domain and Creative Commons-licensed media. Display source credits and copyright information prominently on slides featuring borrowed visuals or data. Verbally acknowledge multimedia creators by name when introducing clips during speeches. Scrupulously honor others' intellectual property and wishes while educating audiences on image authors contributing to your presentation materials.

Crediting Personal Conversations and Interviews

Even personal conversations and interview content require attribution before inclusion in professional public speaking contexts. Always obtain advance permission from individuals before identifying them as sources of quotations or interview insights within speeches. While permission is preferable in writing to avoid future disputes, verbal consent suffices provided it is documented somehow, like recorded while obtaining it. Protect personal contacts by anonymizing sensitive details, potentially inviting harassment or privacy invasions if made public. Honor transparency, but limit details exposing others unduly.

Adopting Grace When Addressing Citation Errors

Public scrutiny magnifies the pain of source attribution errors. If faced with a legitimate citation oversight or dispute, immediately correct the record sincerely rather than reflexively turning defensive.

Publicly apologize to involved parties, fix omitted attributions, retract unsubstantiated statements, and implement systemic changes to prevent the recurrence of errors. Remember that your broader body of work remains intact regardless of isolated mistakes. Channel the lessons into a deepened commitment to rigorously upholding standards moving forward. Integrity derives from accountability, not perfection.

Respecting Diverse Perspectives

Public speeches giving diverse groups voice command greater attention in our increasingly pluralistic world. This section guides readers in respectfully incorporating diverse perspectives, viewpoints, and experiences into messages through inclusive language, balanced representation, and cultural sensitivity. You will gain strategies for appealing to shared human yearnings across differences. Thoughtful orators avoid alienating swaths of listeners based on identity. Instead, they unite audiences powerfully within a common humanity.

Gender-Inclusive Language Mitigates Stereotypes

Traditional gender-exclusive language like "policemen" or "mankind" subtly perpetuates limited roles and representations. Implement more inclusive word choices referring to people in general neutral terms like "police officers," "humankind," and "they/them." Specify gender only when directly relevant. Similarly, balance examples and anecdotes featuring a diverse mix of girls, boys, women, and men rather than defaulting to males. Language evolves along with culture. Monitor speech patterns to phase out unintentional exclusionary holdovers embedding restrictive stereotypes.

Multicultural Examples Build Empathy Bridges

Vivid storytelling captivates audiences, but cultural references should resonate equally with listeners from varied backgrounds. Seek engaging anecdotes featuring diverse names, cultural traditions, foods, music, and dress. Research celebratory events and holidays meaningful to minority groups you can incorporate as examples.

Survey global news for issues concerning marginalized communities to reference thoughtfully. Draw from voices beyond your own experience. Multicultural allusions send the meta-message that your speech welcomes and values everyone's presence. Thoughtful inclusion inspires.

Balance Representation Conscientiously

As public attention grows regarding diversity, speakers risk viewing historically marginalized groups as mere tokens obligatorily mentioned to satisfy expectations. Audiences notice shallow representation. Instead, dedicate time proportionally to issues affecting minorities' lives and voices beyond cursory references.

Seek their input to incorporate authentic concerns and diverse viewpoints upfront in shaping speech content. If highlighting specific groups, share detailed, nuanced explorations of their humanity versus cursory caricatures. Genuine representation embodies true respect, not box-checking.

Research Cultural Contexts thoroughly

Insufficient cultural understanding breeds insensitive misrepresentation. Invest extensive background research before incorporating another community into speeches, especially if little firsthand experience exists.

Explore lived cultural contexts, values, concerns, opinions, and taboos through books, documentaries, and interviews to avoid projecting assumptions ignorantly. Quote group advocates to convey perspectives accurately in their own voices. Vet potentially controversial speech sections with trusted group members to identify issues. While it is impossible to understand every culture equally, make good-faith efforts to portray groups appropriately through context research.

Embracing Shared Humanity and Values

Some cultural divides seem vast, especially amid heated rhetoric exploiting fears of the "other." However, emphasizes shared human yearnings and values bridging divisions. Note common life milestones all celebrate or honors bestowed regardless of background. Highlight universal themes in diverse art and literature. Avoid politics and third rails. Instead, focus on common ground like cherishing children, helping neighbors, taking pride in work, and dreaming big. Shared humanity remains. Eloquent speakers summon people's better angels, not darker demons that divide. What unites us eclipses labels meant to polarize.

Ethical Persuasion and Influence

Public speakers wield immense power to influence listeners' attitudes, decisions, and actions through persuasive words. However, with such influence comes grave responsibility.

This section guides readers in ethically utilizing proven persuasion techniques like appeals to emotion, reciprocity, authority, and repetition. You will gain strategies to persuade audiences through inspiration and logic while avoiding manipulation or deception. Respect for listener agency and dignity should govern every choice.

Transparency of Speaker Self-Interest

While persuasion aims to influence audiences, speakers should remain transparent regarding self-interests possibly shaping their positions. Disclose any financial, ideological, professional, or personal stakes you may hold regarding the persuasive argument's outcome.

Making interests explicit allows listeners to weigh information and be aware of possible motivating biases rather than feeling duped later. However, stop short of over-apologizing or undermining your own credibility upfront. Full disclosure combined with still confidently presenting evidence strengthens your case.

Factually Correct Representations

Building strong rational cases bolsters ethical arguments more than distorting facts conveniently. Ensure representations accurately reflect objective documented evidence rather than cherry-picked or dubiously sourced statistics warped to fit agendas. Cite recent reputable studies supporting claims and provide full context. Admit the limitations of your perspective and data unknowns. While passion can be persuasive emotionally, keep representations grounded in factual accuracy. Truth builds trust.

Appealing to Listeners' Noble Values

Cynical persuaders play to audiences' worst impulses like greed, anger, or prejudice. Appeal instead to people's highest principles like justice, compassion, courage, and community. Frame proposals around expanding fairness, opportunity, empathy, responsibility, freedom, security, or progress. Avoid fueling divisiveness and contempt.

With idealism and honesty, most audiences will thoughtfully weigh appeals aligned with noble values they uphold, provided you respect differing conceptions of virtue. Persuasion elevates when avoiding manipulation.

Empowering Audience Agency

Persuasion should inspire audiences toward positive choices through their own agency, not pressure tactics imposing your will. Supplement passionate appeals with rational data for individuals to weigh and assess individually. Suggest ideal outcomes while acknowledging realistic constraints requiring compromise. Outline action options at varying commitment levels. But allow people space to decide what behavior changes or sacrifices they sustainably pledge vs. burning out through coercion. The most enduring persuasion equips people to voluntarily adopt evolved thinking themselves.

Consenting to Ethical Persuasion

Powerful emotional persuasion can impact listeners' lives profoundly. Therefore, ensure audiences expect and consent to being persuaded through advanced disclosure by organizers or in the communication of event purposes. Make participation voluntary by allowing people to leave without consequence. Seek commitment only to changes individuals can morally accept upon thoughtful reflection.

Avoid artificially trapping or pressuring listeners against their ultimate will. Persuasion shrouded in deception manipulates. But transparency allows even vivid appeals to flow from positive choices.

CHAPTER 11

Public Speaking as a Career

Public speaking is not just a valuable life skill – it can also be a viable career path. Many skilled communicators now make a living through public speaking as demand grows for dynamic speakers who can inspire, educate, and motivate diverse audiences. This chapter explores public speaking as a professional career option and provides guidance on how to build a successful speaking business.

Exploring Professional Opportunities

Public speaking offers a wide range of professional engagement opportunities. Here are some of the most common roles that public speakers take on:

Corporate Training and Workshop Facilitation

Corporate training involves delivering workshops, presentations, and seminars to employees, managers, and other organizational staff. Training topics include technical skill development, leadership, team building, customer service, and more. Public speakers contract with companies to facilitate engaging workshops and sessions.

Developing Training Content

Speakers work closely with client companies to understand their training needs when undertaking a corporate training contract. This involves researching to analyze gaps in employee knowledge or skills. Speakers will design pre-training surveys and assessments to baseline existing understanding. They also study organizational strategies, initiatives, and goals to align training programs. Detailed training briefs capture all objectives that content must fulfill.

Customizing for the Target Audience

Effective training customization requires thorough profiling of attendees. Speakers analyze audience demographics like department, role, tenure, location, and past training history. They also understand organizational culture and workplace nuances. Personas are developed to represent common attendee archetypes. This process ensures topics, language, and examples directly resonate. Audiences with diverse backgrounds may require completely distinct content approaches and delivery styles.

Designing Interactive Training Sessions

To maximize engagement and retention, corporate training sessions incorporate various interactive elements. Speakers choose from a toolkit including icebreakers, group discussions, role plays, simulations, case studies, visual analogies, polls, and quizzes tailored for topics. Technology like slide polling apps increases participation in virtual training. Sessions achieve objectives through diverse activities that cement new skills and knowledge beyond lectures.

Producing Support Materials

Training programs leverage collateral, including workbooks, digital handouts, video clips, assignment instructions, and more. Speaker's source or create multimedia aligned with specific topics at varying depths. Reference materials reinforce key takeaways for post-training applications and assessments. Tools aid different learning styles and provide optional deep dives for motivated learners.

Assessing Program Effectiveness

To demonstrate ROI and value to clients, speakers implement comprehensive evaluation strategies. Pre and post-training surveys capture shifts in attitudes and understanding levels. Practice assessments evaluate the application of new capabilities. Long-term follow-ups track ongoing impact and success stories over weeks/months. Feedback drives continuous enhancement of speaker expertise and future program refining.

Facilitator Skills and Trainer Certification

Facilitating impactful corporate training requires mastery over soft skills like engaging various personalities, managing group dynamics, adapting spontaneously, and maintaining energy over full-day sessions. Formal instructor certification programs instill research-backed techniques for teaching adults and maintaining training rigor.

Keynote Speaking at Conferences and Events

Many conferences, conventions, exhibitions, and corporate events hire professional keynote speakers to deliver an inspirational or thought-provoking opening or closing address. Speakers are chosen based on their expertise in areas relevant to the event theme and industry.

Vetting Event Opportunities

Speakers consider various factors when evaluating keynote proposals. They analyze event agendas to ensure their area of focus aligns with the overall conference. Logistics like travel requirements, length of speech, and audiovisual support are also important. Compensation levels are weighed against time invested in customizing content.

Researching Event Organizers

Thorough research into event organizers is crucial. Speakers visit websites to understand organizer missions and past speaker lineups. This provides context on the type of presentations valued previously. Connecting with event leads on LinkedIn reveals further background. Firsthand attendee referrals and organizer testimonies validate opportunities.

Crafting Customized Proposals

Professional keynote proposals reflect a deep knowledge of the specific event, goals, and anticipated audience. Speakers highlight how their expertise perfectly answers the most pressing questions attendees seek to resolve. Tentative speech outlines provide a taste of the experience without giving away full content. The proposal style mirrors the organizers' business formality.

Rehearsing and Fine-Tuning

Once booked, speakers rehearse presentations extensively, timing delivery and practicing transitions between diverse content types. Feedback from pilot audience runs improves dialogue and story relatability. Advanced technology needs are stress-tested. Last-minute adjustments incorporate any contextual updates enhancing speech relevance on-site.

Pre-Event Consultations

Valuable intel emerges from organizers covering anticipated attendance numbers, venue layouts, introduction protocols, and any special requests. Relationships established over multiple consultations foster familiarity for the optimal onsite experience. Event hashtags and promotional guidelines clarify speakers' social media involvement.

Motivational Speaking to a Variety of Audiences

Motivational speakers share inspiring life stories and lessons through energizing, entertaining speeches. They appear at conferences, corporate off-sites, school/college assemblies, and nonprofit fundraisers.

Developing Signature Stories

At the heart of every motivational presentation lies a poignant true story from the speaker's personal journey. Speakers meticulously craft focused narratives highlighting turning points, challenges overcome, lessons learned, and results achieved to engage any audience emotionally. Stories evolve based on context but retain authenticity.

Incorporating Humor

Motivational speeches maintain high energy through strategic, appropriate Humor tailored for each unique setting and culture. Stories integrate relatable, funny anecdotes that enhance lessons and create lasting memories. Jokes never undermine the overall impactful message or offend. Wry quips keep long speeches lively.

Closing the Engagement Loop

Calls to action challenge listeners to apply insights through specific next steps to improving lives and communities. Speakers skillfully elicit commitments and distribute action plans without coming across as preachy. Contact details facilitate post-event follow-through. Leveraging organizational networks multiplies a speech's after-effects.

Matching Speeches to Each Occasion

Program concepts vary considerably by industry, demographic priorities, and event goals. Motivational specialists curate response banks covering countless adaptive niche presentations. Careful screening ensures only the perfectly aligned option leads to any occasion.

Crafting Supporting Materials

Booklets, videos, and digital handouts expand on key ideas and action plans for ongoing support. Affordable options maximize accessibility. Speakers consider bundling materials with future coaching packages or online courses to extend transformation.

Monitoring Long-Term Impact

Gathering six-week and annual impact surveys from past hosts gauges true differences made. Featured success stories showcase real change on speakers' social platforms, boosting credibility and referrals. Ongoing impact fuels continuous refining of high-ROI motivational formulas.

Consulting and Coaching for Public Speakers

Experienced public speakers often become consultants, advising other speakers, entrepreneurs, and professionals on presentation skills, speechwriting, personal branding, and business development.

One-on-One Speaker Coaching

Private, customized coaching packages help individual speakers hone their craft and business acumen. Consultants conduct in-depth assessments to identify strengths and development areas. Action plans nurture specific skills through individual or buddy practice, feedback sessions, curated resources, and check-ins. Packages vary in intensity and duration.

Group Workshop Facilitation

Interactive skills-building workshops bring efficiency to speaker training. Topics include storytelling, extemporaneous speaking, persuasive techniques, networking, and more. Modules feature mini-lessons, brainstorming, guided activities, peer reviews, and takeaways. Scheduling flexibility accommodates partners.

Keynote and Training Program Consulting

For premium clients, consultants collaborate intensively on entire program builds from concept to delivery. This ensures flawless customization, structure, flow, and reinforcement of key messages to maximize influence. Consultants act as sounding boards, devil's advocates, and mirrors to enhance program impact.

Online Course and Program Development

Leveraging online modalities diversifies revenue streams. Consultants Create in-depth online courses integrating bite-sized video lessons, quizzes, assignments, and community forums. Programming advances at individual paces complemented by coaching options. Affordability expands access to training globally.

Public Speaking Assessments

Structured assessments identify strengths and weaknesses and customize development paths for speakers. Detailed quantitative and qualitative analysis examines materials, presence, speech mechanics, and business practices. Multi-rater feedback incorporates observer perspectives.

Keynote Critiquing Services

Pilot presentations receive intensive critiques from consulting teams experienced in success attributes various client verticals covet most. Objective feedback and brainstorming bolster content, delivery innovations, and client value considerably.

Teaching Public Speaking Courses and Programs

College and university faculty and private institutes hire speakers with distinguished careers to teach public speaking courses. Curricula may cover fundamentals, advanced techniques, and specialty areas like persuasive speaking.

Designing Course Blueprints

Educators design curricula balancing theory and practical application. Learning objectives, assessments, projects, and syllabi systematically progress skills. Backward course planning aligns lessons logically toward program-level proficiency.

Developing Lesson Plans

Detailed lesson plans bring curricula to life interactively. Educators choose pedagogical methods like mini-lectures, demonstrations, discussions, peer workshops, and multimodal activities suited to topics and learning contexts. Asynchronous options support diverse schedules.

Facilitating Student Development

Formative feedback and coaching propel each student incrementally. Speeches receive actionable reviews while nurturing confidence. Educators model nuanced skills and troubleshoot challenges personally. Mentorship inspires continued growth beyond courses.

Assessing Program Effectiveness

Impact assessments evaluate learning outcomes comprehensive of skills, mindsets, and continued application. Qualitative surveys capture attitude shifts and qualitative reflections. Professional portfolios demonstrate capstone-level work and program-level proficiency.

Corporate Emceeing and Master of Ceremonies Roles

Corporations hire skilled emcees and masters of ceremonies to smoothly facilitate conferences, award shows, product launches, and other major events.

Event Planning Involvement

Savvy MCs participate in planning stages, interfacing with stakeholders to thoroughly understand event intent, flow, protocols, and contingencies like technical difficulties. Their guidance enhances the experience's polish.

Greeting Attendees

Charismatic on-site hosting begins at arrivals, where MCs warmly engage all present, boosting camaraderie and excitement for the day/night ahead. Name tagging, programs, and Spot-answering establish accessibility.

Building a Personal Brand as a Public Speaker

Developing a clear personal brand is crucial for public speakers to market themselves effectively and build a professional reputation. Here are some key aspects of crafting a distinctive speaking brand:

Defining Your Niche and Expertise

The first step involves deep self-reflection on experiences, passions, and core strengths that set you apart. Researching popular industry niches provides insights into opportunities while highlighting gaps a new niche could fill. By studying target audiences, speakers further understand specific needs left unmet within industries or topics their unique backgrounds position them to impact. Focusing on a niche allows tailoring content and messaging to attract ideal clients seeking solutions within that scope.

Developing industry expertise requires ongoing dedication to staying knowledgeable on advancements and trends. Speakers research continuously, leverage networks for intel, and pursue professional development-enhancing competencies. They contribute to the field through additional content, research, and impacted community involvement, reinforcing authorities within their focused niche. Strong niche identities boost client confidence that speakers fully grasp issues and deliver maximum value.

Crafting Your Speaker Positioning Statement

A positioning statement crystallizes a brand's promise in a few memorable sentences. Effective statements specify the niche served before affirming core strengths or experiences differentiating the brand. They then directly address critical audience pain points the brand uniquely resolves through speeches, programs, or additional services. Lastly, a tangible call to action motivates prospects to explore opportunities for collaboration immediately.

Well-crafted positioning statements remain concise yet compelling. Refinement requires routinely examining the impact on target clients to ensure resonating relevance. Testing statements across diverse channels and formats aid refinement until precisely distilling the brand's essence and advantages in a balanced, benefits-driven way, attracting ideal partnerships. Consistent reinforcing across all marketing maintains top-of-mind awareness.

Developing Signature Speeches

Signature presentations anchored in expertise exemplify a brand while captivating prospects and audiences. Outlines start by identifying an urgent industry issue or opportunity. Compelling narratives, frameworks, and multimedia transport audiences through enlightening, impactful journeys resolving that focus.

Speakers solicit refinements from pilot audiences representing future clients. Alternative phrasings, modified structures, and enhanced visual aids continually improve the capture and fulfillment of target expectations. Well-honed signature speeches yield proposals ready to seal deals spotlighting unmatched value. Ongoing tweaking maintains alignment with evolving landscapes while retaining core messages and attracting devoted followers.

Building an Online Presence and Assets

A professional online portfolio introduces brands through high-quality, regularly-updated channels. Websites act as digital business cards, while social platforms spark meaningful conversations. Together, these presences showcase thought leadership and generate opportunities directly and indirectly.

Beyond basic profiles, bios, and headshots, websites house optimized writings, manuals, webinars, and other lead magnets. Analytic insights guide strategic optimizing for qualified traffic and conversions. Active social media shares valuable contributions without overt promotions damaging credibility. Consistency bolsters reputation and accessibility anywhere, anytime. Multimedia uploads augment experiences for distance discovery and virtual networking.

Publishing Articles, Books, and Additional Content

Impactful content expands spheres of influence and reach within search results. Before publishing, speakers clearly defined goals like lead generation versus community education. They consider high-traffic outlets or curated compilations most appropriately promoting their niche authorities to attract ideal partnerships.

First-hand industry perspectives provide value while humanizing brands as reliable resources. Topics reflect core competencies and audience interests while solving pressing problems succinctly. Quality, originality, and consistency over time cement reputations for visionary thought leadership justifying premium positioning. All content connects prospects directly back to primary information sources and call-to-actions.

Networking Within Industry Circles

Engagement across complementary professional networks nurtures opportunities organically. Speakers identify conferences and associations aligning with specialties to participate meaningfully through content contributions, committee involvement, and relationship-building. Select panel discussions and hosted events elevate visibility and trust within circuits.

Strategic partnerships bring mutual strengths together for collaborative campaigns. Speakers approach qualified allies respectfully to explore high-potential synergies like cross-promotions, codeveloped programs, or shared client rosters. Arrangements maximize impacts while minimizing solo efforts. Together, partnerships amplify the reach of consistently complementary messages and offerings.

Managing Online Reviews and Testimonials

Authentic endorsements from satisfied clients and audiences substantiate value and build confidence in uncertain prospects. Speakers actively solicit and curate positive feedback, prominently featured on marketing sites. Transparent ratings and sorted comments showcase widespread impacts. Testimonials spark intrigue and preempt challenges by addressing concerns upfront through social proof.

Regular surveying also uncovers areas for improvement addressed sincerely. Any issues receive swift, considerate handling to rescue reputations. Overall, proactive management presents brands as dedicated to continual upgrades informed by all stakeholders for optimal collaborations along smooth journeys. Strong reviews accumulate autonomously over time from raving fans and referrals.

Marketing and Networking for Speaking Engagements

Securing regular paid engagements requires tireless multi-pronged marketing and networking customized to brand attributes and goals. Here are effective strategies:

Targeting Ideal Clients and Decision Makers

Thorough research profiles organizations and event types perfectly aligning with areas of specialization. Speakers identify prospect verticals, locations, sizes, cultures, and other criteria for data-driven targeting. Research uncovers key priorities like skills, pain points, and initiatives motivating investments in enriched programs.

Individual stakeholders commissioning tailored solutions become primary foci. Speakers extensively research commissioners' careers, spheres of influence, past events, and organizational roles to deeply understand drivers. Social profiles, articles, and connection histories reveal hot-button issues and frames through which to attract attention via customized value propositions.

Crafting Tailored Speaking Proposals

Targeted proposals showcase a thorough understanding beyond surface details. Speakers highlight intentionally how their niche strengths, signature content, and case studies precisely fulfill prospect needs, stated or unstated. Formats mirror business correspondence styles to blend professionally.

Proposals feature client quotes validating expertise and value. Outlines tease program benefits sans full details, maintaining intrigue. Backlinks amplify social proof and accessibility to extensive credentials. Proposals leverage prospect pain points as a foundation for recommendations, addressing perceptions beforehand.

Cold Calling and Email Outreach

Personal outreach establishes familiarity where a brand is unknown to decision-makers. Speakers craft direct, value-first communications referencing any warm introductions when possible. Prepared unique virtual meet requests following brief phone introductions for rapport-building and need-validating discussions.

Follow-up customized proposals arrive promptly, addressing discussion takeaways. Periodic reconnects periodically reference prior discussions respectfully while providing updates on fresh insights of potential interest. Positive, solution-oriented tones cultivate relationships throughout exploratory dialogues.

Submitting to Speaking Bureaus

Major bureaus unlock exposure far exceeding solo efforts. Detailed multimedia profiles showcase brands compellingly within easy search filters. Speakers regularly update accomplishments, insights, and program descriptions reflecting expertise maturation to maintain relevance.

Connecting frequently through bureau communications and matchmaker services expedites consideration. Sponsoring bureaus' conferences exponentially grows brand awareness among affiliates and clients. Submissions directly address bureau mission alignment for prioritization.

Targeting Event Planning Associations

Valuable intelligence emerges from trade associations' databases and event directories. Research targets regional chapters and national conferences aligned with signature speeches. Speakers approach programming chairs personally and inquire about interest by sharing a program overview, availability, and flexible pricing.

Volunteering for lesser programming roles like moderation or panels builds familiarity unobtrusively. Producing relevant association content earns influence among key planners and power brokers for preferential access to iconic events launching careers.

Attending Industry Conferences

On-site networking expands brand exposure to countless qualified stakeholders under one roof. Sessions provide a firsthand understanding of issues motivating event investments. Speakers circulate professional collateral and business cards while engaging attendees through insightful conversation.

Capturing attendee lists expedites follow-ups, keeping the momentum flowing digitally. Spearheading conference sessions builds further reputation while exploring fresh partnership and sponsorship options front and center within supportive environments.

Developing Strategic Partnerships

Collaboration maximizes impacts while minimizing individual efforts. Speakers approach compatible businesses and thought leaders, mutually attracting ideal audiences inquiring about how to support missions in high-impact ways. Cross-promotional packages through combined databases and authentic referrals/co-marketing extend all brands' spheres exponentially.

Joint ventures develop like codesigned programs addressing shared passions from various angles, attracting larger, more diverse crowds than possible separately. Partners strategize bundling services creatively for all parties' optimization, such as larger discounts or added value.

PART 2

Exercises and Practice

CHAPTER 12

Confidence-Building Exercises

Public speaking confidence is built gradually over time through consistent practice and experience. While experience speaking in real-world situations is invaluable, it does not always present itself frequently enough for budding public speakers to improve at the desired pace. This is where deliberate confidence-building exercises come into play. Exercises allow you to practice public speaking skills and boost self-assurance in a lower-stakes, learning-focused environment. This chapter will explore some of the most effective confidence-building exercises you can incorporate into your development as a public speaker.

Advanced Visualization Techniques

Visualization is a powerful mental practice that allows you to simulate experiences and condition yourself to respond effectively. Applied to public speaking, advanced visualization techniques can help build confidence from the inside out. Regular visualization cultivates unwavering self-assurance by programming your brain and nervous system to associate speaking with feelings of poise rather than panic. This section will provide extensive guidance on incorporating impactful visualization exercises into your daily routine.

Guided Imagery Scripts

One potent way to leverage visualization's benefits is through guided imagery scripts. These tailored narratives vividly describe ideal speaking situations you can mentally experience. Immersing yourself in guided scripts strengthens your natural ability to self-regulate anxiety and perform at higher levels.

Developing Scripts

The first step is crafting vivid scripts tailored to your needs and speaking goals. Determine contexts requiring the most confidence-building, like technical presentations, conferences, or high-pressure networking. Envision a realistic yet ideal scenario incorporating sensory details. Scripts should follow a chronological sequence of events from preparation through delivering impactful speeches. Provide rich mental pictures of your surroundings, appearance and demeanor, audience reactions, and even feelings of calmness and the ability to think on your feet. Leave room for improvising additional sights, sounds, or scenarios.

Script Components

Effective scripts typically include some key components. Set the stage with visual descriptions of the environment, your attire, and even slight butterflies understood as normal excitement rather than fear. Affirm to yourself that you feel prepared and in control. Once speeches begin, focus on how smooth and proficient your vocal delivery appears. Describe signs of engaged audience interest like nods, smiles, and lack of fidgeting. Envision fielding any post-speech questions with insight, confidence, and even minor Humor. End scripts focusing on positive feelings of accomplishment reinforced by appreciative feedback. Feeling details bring scripts alive.

Using Scripts Effectively

Allot 10-20 minutes minimum daily to visualize scripts vividly. Find a distraction-free spot, relax muscles through deep breathing, and then narrate scripts internally while sensing your imagined reactions. Replay any challenging sections repeatedly until they feel natural. If distractions arise, return focus gently without judgment. Notice emotional and physical sensations transform as old fears dissipate and a calm, empowered sense of self emerges. Over weeks, neural pathways strengthening this association will manifest through a self-fulfilling prophecy even during real public speaking.

Advanced Scripting Techniques

More involved scripts can solidify new mind-body patterns faster. Record audio versions for participation wherever convenient, like commutes. Role-play scripts in front of a mirror, altering your imagined tone and confidence levels to feel most natural. Actively challenge negative thoughts like "I'll forget my lines" by rehearsing smooth recoveries. Purposefully induce relaxation in visualized scenarios through techniques in section 12.1.5, then observe calmness' impact. Daily scripting cements self-assuredness as an ingrained trait rather than a fleeting mood. Commit to regular practice.

Positive Affirmations

To maximize impact, pair guided visualization with positive self-affirming statements. Affirmations reprogram limiting beliefs, hindering confidence with empowering replacements.

Crafting Effective Affirmations

Well-constructed affirmations should be:

Present-tense ("I speak confidently") rather than future ("I will speak confidently"). Positively phrased, not what you don't want ("I handle interruptions smoothly," not "I won't get flustered"). Emotionally charged to impact subconscious mindset. Specific benefits envisioned include an assured stance, engaging delivery, attentive audiences, and competent answering of questions. Repeated frequently for lasting impact

Incorporating Affirmations

Weave customized affirmations seamlessly into scripts by internally stating them as cue points arise, such as taking the stage or answering questions. Hear and feel the validity of phrases like "My passion for topics radiates assurance" or "I gracefully navigate unpredictables." You can also practice imagery and affirmations separately. Before mirrors, using a confident, carefree tone, say, "I speak powerfully from years of experience" while sensing that level of confidence develop inside. Affirmations condition thoughts supporting confidence.

Additional Affirmation Strategies

Write key phrases on sticky notes visible daily. Record audio versions for listening during commutes. Share reframes respectfully with skeptical friends for accountability. Catch doubts transforming to confident alternatives like "I may get nervous, but channel it positively." Affirm subtle trepidation signs as healthy excitement. Noticing affirmations' impactful ways of shifting internal dialogues empowers wrestling anxieties into aligned versions of self. Commit to consistent usage.

Mental Rehearsal

Another pillar of impactful visualization is mentally rehearsing specific speaking aspects. While guided scripts set idealistic contexts, mental rehearsal focuses on finer details.

Rehearsing Entire Speeches

Without notes, she runs through upcoming speeches in sequential order daily. Hear projected conviction, delivering each point fluidly. Picture audiences' hypnotized focus and occasional nods reinforcing comprehension. Feel yourself thinking nimbly about deviations rather than panicking. See self-confidence emanating palpably. Over weeks, these visualized "lived experiences" condition positive associations supplanting doubts.

Rehearsing Tricky Sections

Zoom focuses on troublesome transitions, key facts, or conclusions precipitating unease. Run such sections repeatedly, envisioning smooth delivery bolstered by preparation rather than inadequacy.

Notice composure strengthens each time. After perfecting tricky elements mentally, real presentation induces less trepidation, knowing you've supposedly "already succeeded."

Mastering Eye Contact

Another crucial yet nerve-wracking art involves maintaining eye contact. Visualize scanning full audiences confidently without fixating uncomfortably long on individuals. See yourself ping-ponging gaze automatically between zones, scanning all engaged faces. Sense ease connecting with crowds through vision rather than wanting to hide behind slides. Regular eye contact rehearsal fosters this unconscious fluidity, saving anxiety during the presentation.

Addressing Unexpected Problems

No plan survives first contact with audiences. Anticipate minor issues, mentally rehearsing poised solutions. For instance, envision projecting confidence and recovering smoothly from brief lapses rather than frustration. Or see the charm in lightly acknowledging a genuine audience question you'd misplaced facts for, then honestly and humbly clarifying respectfully. Regularly practicing composure amid minor deviations neurologically programs flexibility and presence of mind when unpredictables inevitably emerge.

Mental rehearsal gives the invaluable experience of "living through" ideal speaking scenarios countless times. Its cumulative impact cultivates unshakable reservoirs of inner poise accessible whenever spotlights shine. Commit to incorporating regular rehearsal into daily routines.

Progressive Muscle Relaxation

Physical relaxation techniques complement other visualization strategies by relaxing anxiety's hold on the body. Tension undermines poise, so regular relaxation exercise starves the negative physiology of fuel.

Guiding Progressive Muscle Relaxation

Begin seated comfortably or lying down. Starting from your toes, tightly curl, then relax muscles sequentially upwards through calves, thighs, hips, abdominal region, chest, shoulders, arms, neck, and face whilst maintaining easy breathing. Hold the tension for 5-10 seconds before each slow release, accompanied by exhaling fully. Notice how tension dissolves with each group. Repeat periodically relaxing fully before starting the next section to deepen benefits.

Advanced PMR Techniques

For more involvement, muscularly enact scenarios requiring poised states. Step onto a stage feeling your legs light yet grounded. Square shoulders relaxed yet powerful. Lift chin confidently while softening facial tension. Enliven hands ready to gesticulate freely without constraint. Breathe easy access to inner assurance. Also, combine deep relaxation visualization, such as standing before a mirror and slowly sinking deeper into a safe, stress-free space with each breath out. Still, the mind.

Benefits of Regular Practice

Physiological relaxation chips away at tensions underpinning performance anxieties over weeks. Regular PMR induces calm before speeches and conditions your autonomic nervous system, favoring relaxation in response to speaking cues versus stress. This reframes public situations as opportunities instead of ordeals while maximizing poise potential. Making relaxation habitual supports flourishing self-assuredness.

Public Speaking Workshops and Courses

While visualization builds confidence internally, external practice environments provide unparalleled opportunities to develop speaking skills experimentally. Workshops and courses cultivate assurance through a supportive yet challenging crucible of repetitive practice, feedback application, and incremental growth. This section explores structured training options and best practices for maximizing their confidence-boosting impact.

Introductory Courses

Community colleges and adult education programs commonly offer beginner public speaking courses ideal for novices. Contact local options to fit schedules.

Course Components

Most intro courses follow similar formulas. Curricula break down speaking fundamentals methodically through mini-lessons, exercises, and low-stakes presentations. Expect addressing speech organization, verbal delivery techniques, controlling anxiety, active listening skills, and oral communicating fundamentals. Diverse classmates foster safe yet inspirational environments encouraging initiation.

Maximizing Intro Course Benefits

Review lessons thoroughly and practice constantly outside class. Journal anxieties to normalize them as excitement or note progress. Recognize successes rather than fixating solely on flaws. Approach each speech as an opportunity rather than an evaluation. After presenting, actively solicit classmate feedback beyond instructors to diversify perspectives. Apply multiple recommendations simultaneously rather than becoming overwhelmed. Celebrate triumphing over fears step-by-step to reinforce intrinsic motivation.

Beyond the Classroom

Map out trajectories for continuing confidence-building like Toastmasters. Find speaking colleagues enthusiastically supporting one another's progressions. Swap recorded practice presentations critiquing respectfully via video calls. Create flashcard decks condensing memorization tips. Teach concepts learned to family, maintaining knowledge through instruction. Review syllabi periodically, rekindling sparks motivating continuous growth. Pass skills forward, paying knowledge dividends.

Intro courses cultivate comfort through instilling basics yet leave immense room remaining. Commit to maximizing learning's lasting impacts.

Toastmasters

Toastmasters provides unparalleled structured speaking development worldwide. Members swear by its incremental, long-haul confidence cultivation.

Club Components

Meetings emulate real-world speaking through timed role-playing, impromptu speaking, formal presentations, and leadership roles. Assignments systematically build skills through Toastmasters' educational programs, teaching new methods bimonthly. Experienced coaches guide speeches and constructively critique performances respectfully yet insightfully via systematized feedback forms.

Gaining the Most from Membership

Attend faithfully, fitting obligations into schedules. Treat assignments seriously with preparation beyond minimal requirements. Position oneself vulnerably by regularly volunteering taller orders, pushing personal boundaries gradually rather than waiting passively assigned. Of course, endeavor learning roles like toastmaster or grammarian also grants new confident perspectives. Solicit mentorship from accomplished members. Record presentations carefully, self-critiquing honestly afterward as well.

Long-Term Commitment Rewards

Stick diligently to paths, lowering fears step-by-step rather than burning out. Celebrate small wins, keeping motivation fiery. Over the years, fear gradually fades, replaced by abilities addressing increasingly complex scenarios brimming with self-assuredness. Toastmasters cultivate speaking agency through patience and repetition under skilled guidance beyond any other option. Its structured yet flexible formula works provided steadfast dedication.

Public speaking mastery emerges through perpetual progress. Remain actively engaged, continually practicing and learning within supportive communities.

Intensive Workshops

For rapid yet compressed confidence development, intensive half-day to weeklong workshops offer immersive alternatives to accessing field-leading expertise.

Program Components

Curricula focus intensely on techniques debunking excuses, anchoring assured states, desensitizing to anxiety triggers, and polishing poise under pressure. Short yet frequent speeches before coaching receive thorough personalized feedback. Role-playing simulated pressure-cooker scenarios strengthens responding calmly rather than choking. Video-recording speeches allow objective self-analysis reinforcing lessons.

Maximizing Intensive Impact

Arrive having visualized oneself completing intensive with newly found confidence reservoirs. Soak up every advice nugget by participating fully rather than procrastinating exercises. After workshops, schedule follow-up simulations rehearsing resilience before reverting to doubts. Review recordings noting assured qualities are emerging versus former self-critiquing respectfully. Apply wisdom daily, preventing skills erosion through consistent speaking situations, eventually mastered with poise.

Choosing Effective Programs

Select workshops proven to empower others via research-backed techniques from field experts. Probe instructor portfolios, ascertaining depth and helping diverse profiles. Programs should streamline thriving under stressors rather than performatively preaching techniques. Intensives optimize confidence explosions, accessing expertise concentrated yet flexible and retaining skills indefinitely with diligent follow-through.

Structured speaking development cultivates assurance through long-term learning yet intensively accelerating maturation, compressing wisdom. Seek constant practice accompanied by supportive environments, maximizing all opportunities. Commit fully to getting the most from transformative experiences.

Advanced Workshops

For confidence-building newly inspired levels, delve deeper into specialized applications.

Specialized Content Immersion

Workshops target narrowly defined contexts like technical presentations, sales pitches, or conference speaking. Curricula intensively cover strategies, cerebrally sharpen applicable expertise, and provide realistic simulations polishing poise within specializations.

Mentorship Programs

Some programs formally pair with an experienced speaker coaching customized development. Regular check-ins and feedback sessions strengthen skillsets, tailoring guidance to personal improvement pathways. Commitment reaps proficiency and assurance, surpassing solitary study.

Executive Presence Intensives

Multi-day workshops transform presence for C-suite professionals. Immersing deeply into projecting composure and gravitas under Wall Street pressure levels through personalized coaching and high-stakes simulations boosts careers exponentially.

Collegiate Speech and Debate Programs

For students seeking intensive collegiate-level training, competitive speech and debate programs offer rigorous immersion.

Program Components

Coursework covers advanced oratory, argumentation, cross-examination, and rhetorical analysis. Students participate in regional and national tournaments, presenting speeches and engaging in competitive debates against other collegians. Experienced coaches provide individualized mentoring.

Benefits of Public Speaking Development

The competitive environment challenges students to hone skills under pressure rapidly. Winning invitational tournaments requires poise and effectively articulating complex ideas before scrutinizing judges. Video review sessions identify even subtle ways to boost stage presence and delivery. Years of debate experience leave graduates exceptionally equipped with the confidence to advocate positions persuasively in any professional domain.

Maximizing the Collegiate Experience

Commit fully to daily practicing beyond minimal classwork. Voluntarily take on leadership roles organizing tournaments. Record and scrutinize speeches regularly, identifying nuanced skill adjustments. Proactively solicit intensive one-on-one coaching from staff. After graduation, remain engaged by coaching younger teams or judging debates. Translating debate training into long-term presentation forms retains limitless benefits.

Specialized Conference Training

For professionals presenting at important sector conferences, pre-conference intensives prime polish.

Training Components

These workshops focus on optimizing conference talk delivery through rehearsal, review sessions, and dynamic role-plays. Key topics include making research accessible to non-experts, fielding rigorous Q&A confidently, and optimizing the all-important optics to create a memorable presence.

Catalyzing Career Growth

Conference speaking represents a prime opportunity for growing reputations and networks. Thus, these intensives catalyze assurance, making the most of such visibility. Practicing with field experts keeps nervousness at bay, allowing full charisma to channel into idea dissemination and connecting. Outcomes often include new professional doors opening.

High-Stakes Simulations and Role-Playing

While visualization and courses supply foundational skills, realistically simulating pressure-cooker situations provides unparalleled preparation. Performing before live audiences induces nerves, yet role-playing removes consequences, allowing focus on craft rather than fears. This section provides extensive guidance on conducting impactful simulations and strengthening poisedness.

Mock Conference Presentations

Simulating conference talks before colleagues mimics stakes inspiring peak performance. Producing polished research conveys competence-boosting careers.

Recruiting Roles

Beyond presenter, assign skeptic colleagues roles like dismissive conference attendees covertly texting, combative questioners challenging every statement, and loud sidebar talkers distracting from points. Others act as event coordinators, session chairs, or live-streamed audience surrogates.

Planning an Effective Simulation

Provide background materials in advance, allowing roles time to characterize authentically. Designate rehearsal blocks with role-players receiving orientation on accentuating pressure intensities realistically yet respectfully. Presenters prepare thoroughly, visualizing composure amid unexpected criticisms. Videotape sessions allow review pinpointing even subconscious mannerism adjustments bolstering poise.

After-Action Review

Debrief constructively, noting exemplary moments and maintaining flow versus stumbling factors. Discussed anxieties and strategies for conquering pressures effectively. Celebrate resilience emerging with each successive simulation refining prowess. Applying accrued wisdom retains mastery indefinitely. Seeing setbacks as learning instead of failure fuels continuous improvement cycles.

Advanced Scenarios

Spice subsequent simulations unpredictably represent increasingly realistic stakes. For example, present cutting-edge findings risk rival appropriation, necessitating rapid defenses. Or present amid equipment failures, compelling improvisation strengthening adaptability. Constantly challenging comfort zones cultivate steadiness, conquering any contingency.

Consistent mock conferences systematically desensitize fears while polishing researcher panache-inspiring respect. Committing to these intense crucibles stamps authority, permanently diminishing the possibility of choking under scrutiny.

Mock Job Interviews

Authentic practice facing hiring managers and competitors sharpens poise in securing dream careers. Confidence sells oneself most effectively.

Recruiting Panelists

Source established professional colleagues role-playing interviewers realistically. Assign diverse archetypes like overbearing micromanagers, disconnected elitists, and attentive yet scrutinizing evaluators. Provide background reviews, allowing thorough characterization.

Planning Authentic Simulations

Designate private interview spaces resembling real settings. Develop interview guides, including behavioral and technical questions highlighting strengths yet uncovering weaknesses. Schedule mock interviews at periodic intervals mirroring real pacing. Consider post-interview networking simulations also strengthening assuredness.

Applying Valuable Feedback

Videotape sessions for review jointly critiquing communication and qualifying strengths. Note even subtle mannerism adjustments bolstering presence. Discuss felt anxieties and confident mindsets conquering worries. Contrast successive performances observing resilience strengthening with practice. Internalize accrued wisdom, reshaping narratives highlighting abilities rather than weaknesses.

Realistic Tensions

Spice scenarios reveal competition and interviewing, necessitating convincing hiring managers of differentiation. Or disclose delays compelling improvised small talk displaying interpersonal competence. Constantly stretching ensures thriving under any pressure, demonstrating reasons for selection.

Mock Legal Settings

For aspiring legal professionals, courtroom simulations strengthen eloquence in defending justice under fire.

Assembling Authentic Panels

Court personnel like bailiffs and judges role-play authentically applying jurisprudence mastery. Assign "opposing counsels" aggressively cross-examining utilizing loopholes exposed. Alternatively, recruit Citizen panels acting as juries weighing the plausibility of arguments critically.

Developing Realistic Case Scenarios

Craft case files outlining factual patterns and legal issues. Provide time, allowing thorough preparation. Designate private "courtrooms" emulating atmosphere. Preside over mock trials adjudicating according to proceedings, strengthening rule mastery displayed confidently.

Gaining Invaluable Feedback

Record proceedings are reviewed objectively, noting even subtle weaknesses exploited in compromised cases. Discuss feelings unraveling effective mindsets navigating tensions peacefully. Incremental practice systematically extinguishes courtroom jitters while demonstrating legal sagacity and commanding respect.

Stretching Comfort Zones

Periodically designate "opposing counsel" and prosecuting to strengthen flexibility. Or disclose new evidentiary obstacles compelling on-the-fly adaptation demonstrating resilience. Constantly growing ensures legal lions emerge any contingency with dignity.

Mock Classroom Role-Plays

For educators, role-playing simulations strengthen pedagogical presence managing dynamics.

Recruiting Student Panels

Citizen volunteer panels role-play diverse student archetypes authentically, like distractible back-row talkers, antagonistic contrarians, and engaged over-participators stretching class pacing boundaries.

Planning Immersive Simulations

Provide lesson plans allowing role preparation. Designate private classrooms resembling environments. Moderate mock sessions objectively noting nuanced techniques maintaining order amid unruliness compelling respect.

Gaining Education-Focused Feedback

Record proceedings are reviewed objectively, noting subtle classroom management techniques to maintain order. Note engagement wins cultivating interests versus distraction losses. Gradually strengthen techniques compelling rapt focus despite behaviors.

Strengthening Adaptability

Periodically disclose learning curve alterations like transitional disciplinary problems or modified curricula compelling adaptation demonstrating improvisational expertise. Constant growth cultivates educators thriving in any contingency with dignity.

Business Pitch Role-Plays

For entrepreneurs, role-playing simulations strengthen assuredness, captivating investors.

Recruiting Investor Panels

Assign colleagues roles like dismissive venture capitalists, meticulous accountants, and enthusiastic yet inexperienced "angel investors" authentically. Provide background reviews, allowing thorough characterization.

Planning Impactful Simulations

Provide thorough business plan drafts and financial projections, allowing meticulous due diligence. Designate private boardrooms emulating investor meetings. Moderate mock sessions provide constructive critiques, strengthening persuasiveness.

Leveraging Valuable Feedback

Record proceedings jointly review pitch finesse, noting even subtle adjustments bolstering charisma. Discussed felt anxieties and confident mindsets overcoming worries wooing backers. Note assurance strengthening with each successive simulation.

Elevating the Pressure

Periodically disclose funding competitors necessitating convictions compelling distinction. Or disclose financial alterations compelling on-the-spot adaptation demonstrating adaptability. Constant growth cultivates entrepreneurs' thriving high-pressure contingencies, impressing investors.

CHAPTER 13

Speech Crafting and Delivery Practice

At this advanced stage in your public speaking journey, it is time to refine your speech writing and delivery skills through deliberate practice. While previous chapters provided foundational knowledge and exercises, this chapter focuses on taking your abilities to the next level. Through targeted techniques and feedback-driven practice, you will emerge as a highly-skilled orator capable of engaging and persuading any audience. Let's begin!

Advanced Speech Writing Techniques

Writing a compelling speech takes more than just researching a topic and outlining major points. Crafting a truly memorable address requires sophisticated writing abilities. In this expanded section, we will delve deeply into numerous advanced speech-writing strategies that will take your speeches to the next level.

Tailoring Your Content to Your Audience

The most effective speeches are tailored specifically to the target audience. Take time to thoroughly research and understand your listeners so you can directly address their interests, concerns, priorities, and level of knowledge on the topic. Customize the content, examples, language, and style of delivery based on who will be in the audience.

Run a short audience survey to gather demographic data on age, industry, experiences, and baseline knowledge. Analyze responses to zero in on what motivates and resonates most with them. Use this information to orient your speech accordingly versus a more generalized approach that may fall flat.

Incorporating Dynamic Storytelling

Stories have a powerful ability to engage listeners and bring dry topics to life. Weave relevant anecdotes, case studies, and narrative examples throughout your speech. Stories should serve to elucidate and exemplify key points while maintaining audience interest.

Develop storytelling skills to transport audiences. Use descriptive imagery and relatable characters/scenarios. Share dramatic turning points and resolution. Embed quotes statistics within stories for authenticity. Practice delivery to achieve storyteller presence through vocal fluctuation, gestures, and eye contact with story subjects. Master story arc and placement to maximize impact.

Crafting a Memorable Introduction

The introduction sets the stage and hooks the audience, so craft it carefully. Capture attention with a compelling opening anecdote, question, statistic, or quote. Clearly state the topic and its importance upfront. Preview your main points to provide structure and satisfy listener expectations.

Brainstorm attention-grabbing hooks on your topic. Refine the best option through practice, gauging timing, and delivery. Tailor quoted sources and stats carefully to resonate with the audience's interests and impact their views on the topic. Ensure preview point titles pique curiosity to actively engage listeners throughout your address.

Structuring the Body Logically

The body of the speech is where you present substantive content. Organize major points and supporting material logically based on principles of order and priority. Common structures include chronological, problem-solution, causal, and topical. Ensure a smooth flow between sections through effective transitions.

Methodically plot how each point will unfold, with the expected duration for sections. Weave in supporting facts and examples at strategic points to enhance understanding and retention of concepts. Carefully craft transitions between sections that move listeners seamlessly through the speech without jarring changes in tone or topic.

Crafting a Persuasive Conclusion

Just as the introduction sets the stage, the conclusion is vital for leaving a lasting impression. Recap main points concisely while emphasizing takeaways. Call listeners to action by clearly stating a specific recommendation or charge. For persuasive speeches, use concluding techniques like reversing order or pulling heartstrings to maximize impact.

Brainstorm calls to action aligned with your topic and audience's motivations. Practice several conclusion options to determine the optimum stimulation of inspiration, motivation, or nod to future involvement. Craft a deathly conclusion that weaves together emotions, key ideas, and your prompt action in a memorable, impactful way, so listeners are excited to apply insights beyond your talk.

Employing Memorable Phrasing

Crafting eloquent, memorable phrasing is an art. Incorporate evocative language that elevates ideas, energizes delivery, and lodges messages firmly in the audience's minds. Study phrases used by great orators across eras for inspiration.

Evaluate your draft for overused phrases you can substitute. Trial new expressions, idioms, and word combinations through practice. Ask peers which phrases stood out and why. Polish final selections for appropriateness, imagery, rhythm when spoken, and inherent persuasiveness. Memorize to give winged delivery that uplifts bigger ideas.

Using Effective Olfactory Language

Vivid descriptive phrases that appeal to senses like sight and smell are highly engaging. Stir the audience's imagination using olfactory adjectives associated with your topic sparingly for impact.

Brainstorm a shortlist of evocative smells linked to your subject. Practice descriptive clauses injecting their subtleties. For example, "The sterile clinical odor permeated patients' rooms as nurses treated endless cases of influenza." Test phrasing on others. Polish selections to harmonize words, painting multi-sensory pictures without distraction. Deploy judiciously for intrigue.

Enlivening Content with Humor

Appropriate humor skillfully employed adds dimension and enjoyment, especially for lighter topics. Look for opportunities to pepper instances of wit, irony, or whimsy through well-timed one-liners or anecdotes to pique interest.

Evaluate jokes or funny stories in your topic area for potential inclusion. Carefully consider audience appropriateness and delivery, practicing timing. Discover your comedic strengths through impromptu humor based on interactions. Maintain control with humor and resume seriousness smoothly. Humor spices up content when used judiciously for fun and rapport.

Considering Visual Presentation Needs

Visual aids, from slides and graphics to props, help audiences follow concepts through multiple learning styles. Assess which presentation tools align with your speech flow and key points for the best impact.

Storyboard your aid types, content, and flow beforehand. Choose tools appropriate to your style that enhance comprehension without distraction. Practice commentary highlighting takeaways. Solicit feedback from mock audiences. Rehearse fluid delivery with visuals, maintaining a connection to live listeners rather than screens. Polish visuals until impactful yet effortless.

Incorporating Alliteration and Devices

Poetic and memorable speech writing employs techniques like parallel construction, alliteration, and rhetorical devices for impact. Study examples from history's great orators to inspire your own use. Experiment with techniques like chiasmus, antithesis, and repetition by practicing short sample passages. Gauge, which devices harmonize with distinct points and overall style. Polish selections through multiple drills, adjusting context as needed. Memorize incorporations to enable the delivery of elevating key ideas. Deploy judiciously for eloquence and memorability.

Proofreading for Perfection

Thorough proofing eliminates glaring errors detracting from the message and credibility. Leave drafts overnight and proof with fresh eyes, reading aloud for flow. Enlist extra proofreaders.

Check for typos, grammatical errors, consistent formatting, and readability. Ensure proper citations and factual accuracy. Tweak phrasing, structure, and supplemental materials. Solicit feedback from others on cohesion and areas needing clarification. Make corrections and get re-approval. Proof to high standards befitting an eloquent, professional product.

Live Audience Practice

Gaining experience speaking in front of live audiences is crucial for developing confidence and delivery abilities. In this expanded section, we'll deeply explore diverse ways to get valuable practice speaking to real people.

Identifying Opportunities in Your Community

Scan your local community for organizations and events seeking speakers. Consider rotary clubs, libraries, senior centers, non-profits, and more. Most will welcome presentations on your expertise or passion. You gain experience while providing value.

Could call organizations to inquire about presenting. Provide your background and the proposed topic's benefits. Follow up in person to build rapport. Join groups like Toastmasters for regular slots. Offer free talks for student/charity events. Get on municipal speaking bureaus. Network constantly and put yourself out there through every connection.

Preparing Thoroughly for Each Gig

Treat every live speaking opportunity as important preparation. Choose an impactful, timely topic and craft your speech with care. Rehearse extensively, refining delivery along the way based on feedback. Prepare visual aids if approved.

Develop signs reminding you of key delivery points backstage. Before speaking, review your script, highlighting transitions, stories, and emotional appeals. Visualize poise and interaction. Practice with presentation tools. Arrive early to acquaint yourself with the venue accommodating speaker needs to avoid anxiety from surprises.

Incorporating Audience Engagement Tactics

Keep listeners involved through engagement tactics like polls, discussions, stories, and demonstrations. Practice making eye contact rather than reading your notes. Invite a few plant questions to start the interaction. Be approachable.

Plan engaging tactics aligned with your content to maximize participation. Foster comforts through humor and smiles. Move purposefully and modulate your voice appealingly. Devote energy to every section of your audience, maintaining connection. Reinforce rapport through eye contact, not just focal points.

Soliciting Constructive Feedback

After each speech, gather feedback to improve. Ask organizers and a few audience members targeted questions about strengths, weaknesses, and ways to enhance impact. Take meticulous notes to analyze later. Elicit specific feedback addressing delivery, content, and room for growth. Note how statements landed, and questions caused confusion. Welcome all perspectives but focus on constructive criticism lending insights. Analyze honestly and create an action plan leveraging strengths while strategizing weaknesses into focused practice areas.

Graduating to Larger Opportunities

As your comfort and skills increase, seek higher-profile opportunities to challenge yourself. Consider presenting to professional organizations, giving TEDx-style talks, or running for local office. Leverage practice to pave the way for larger platforms. Identify organizations conducting conferences fitting your expertise. Propose concise speaking abstracts aligning with their mission. For TEDx events, submit compelling proposals demonstrating experience. Craft speech drafts demonstrating your ability to educate or inspire diverse audiences on vital topics through eloquence and passion.

Creating Branded Online Content

Develop an online presence as a subject matter expert through blogs, videos, and web content. This expands your audience and credentials for larger speaking roles. Select a blog host and establish your online identity. Post consistently on your passion areas while weaving in strategically promoted speaking events. Produce short, informative videos suitable for YouTube and social channels. Utilize multimedia and thought-provoking angles appealing to broad demographics. Build visibility, nurturing your authority.

Approaching Company Events

Corporate conferences, trade shows, and employee training offer exposure to professionals. Approach firms amenable to outside experts on niche topics, improving workforce skills.

Research leading local and national companies aligning with your expertise. Craft short event pitches accentuating ROI from enhanced staff performance or industry insights. Highlight credentials and client endorsements bolstering your value. Follow up established relationships, paving future doors. With practice, exude expertise attracting paid corporate work.

Guest Speaking in Classrooms

Educating students cultivate future audiences and community involvement. Contact schools about guest speaking on specialty topics, supplementing curricula through real-world views. Partner with teachers to plan age-appropriate content. Engage students, maintaining energy and enthusiasm. Employ multimedia, activities, and storytelling compelling young attention spans. Solicit feedback and follow up on opening future invitations. Nurturing youth builds your name recognition and furthers your impact through generations.

Emceeing Local Conferences

Serve as master of ceremonies for regional events to demonstrate public speaking skills. Contact conference directors showcasing your experience and connection to their mission. Emcee duties include introducing sessions smoothly, posing audience polls, and energizing breakouts through humor. Rehearse smooth transitions. Maintain a positive environment radiating warmth from the podium. Meeting speakers backstage eases nerves. Cultivate gratitude for future references. With professionalism, emceeing expands your role, inspiring lifelong affiliations.

Running for Civic Board Positions

Put leadership abilities on display by campaigning for local boards and applying your expertise. Connect your credentials to crucial community issues, energizing potential votes. Craft a compelling candidacy statement highlighting achievements aligning priorities. Conduct outbound calls, emails, and neighborhood meetups to spread your vision. Using digital and guerilla tactics creatively promoting the role of an informed public servant. Should you win a seat, your influence and network will blossom further.

Speaking at Industry Conferences

As skills develop, propose compelling talks at regional tradeshows and conventions connected with professionals. Impress event committees with proposals spotlighting hot topics. Submit well-organized, visually appealing proposals to events aligning with your credentials. Highlight accomplished delivery styles enticing committees. Follow submission rules meticulously. Once accepted, seize the opportunity to leverage remuneration and visibility, spring boarding your stature. Conference circuits bolster prominence through invaluable connections.

Offering Pro Bono Talks for Non-Profits

Provide motivational speeches for charitable causes resonating with your values. Contact leaders were spotlighting complimentary talks inspiring volunteers and donors. Investigate local non-profits addressing meaningful issues. Craft timely proposals accentuating how your presentation uplifts stakeholders through fresh perspectives on overcoming adversity or cultivating compassion. Strengthen goodwill while refining delivery, touching souls.

Guest Lecturing at Universities

Approach colleges to share expertise and inspire the next generations. Solicit department heads regarding guest speaking slots, furthering curricula with practical views. Contact schools showcasing transcripts documenting achievements. Highlight experience imparting knowledge through memorable talks energizing learning. Propose enticing, well-researched topics augmenting coursework. Bring passion, igniting fledgling minds. Form bonds offering future guidance.

Hosting Online Video Series

Launch an instructional video podcast or YouTube series to spread your insights virally. Develop episode topics through ongoing contributor value. Invest in quality equipment and soundproofing. Scout video hosts. Draft episode outlines exploring angles intriguing to novices and experts alike. Promote extensively boosting subscribers. Disseminating knowledge far and wide. Monetize later through ads or paid content.

Approaching Local Media Outlets

Contact television, radio, and print, pursuing interview slots showcasing expertise on current events. Provide exceptional value through clever angles on important issues. Draft media pitches encapsulating hot topics concisely. Highlight credentials qualifying you as a thoughtful source. Follow meticulous formatting and deadlines. Demonstrate charisma, authority, and likeability if selected. Leverage clips growing name recognition and future invites. Media magnifies influence endlessly.

Entering Speech Competitions

Compete locally and nationally, honing competitive techniques. Research categories align with strengths while stimulating continued growth. Identify events evaluating eloquence, structure, and persuasive brilliance. Craft compelling, finely-honed speeches meeting guidelines. Rehearse extensively. With placements, acclaim leads to coaching roles uplifting fellow orators. Competitions accelerate mastery through public scrutiny.

Speaking at Leadership Retreats

Motivate executives through impactful talks centered on resilience, vision, and collaboration at secluded corporate gatherings. Contact HR leaders highlighting persuasive strengths energizing high-caliber minds. Craft proposals are accentuating tangible takeaways supporting strategic objectives. Deliver with passion, inspiring lasting change. Cultivate esteem-building re-invites fueling your renown. Retreats magnetize heavy hitters, amplifying clout.

Volunteering as Toastmasters Mentor

Give back shared expertise, guiding others through Toastmasters leadership positions and cultivating camaraderie. Having mastered meeting roles, contact district directors proposing a coaching role. Guide members in crafting speeches and adjudicating with care, empathy, and constructive feedback. Foster risk-taking, propelling all to new heights. Rewarding relationships reap future platforms upon their success. Mentorship nourishes personal fulfillment.

Teaching Public Speaking Workshops

Impart years of knowledge, helping novices level up through interactive classes. Craft curricula maximize takeaways. Contact community centers, libraries, plus employer training departments. Develop dynamic, multifaceted syllabi that inspire attendees. Leverage speech samples, activities, and feedback. Maintain enthusiasm, energizing every learner. Witnessing growth brings fulfillment, establishing your teaching career. Instructional workshops expand impressive repute.

Creating an Online Speaking Agency

Launch a virtual agency booking talks, developing content, and coaching clients to global stages with your team of experts. Incorporate with mission cultivating confidence in others. Craft service offerings meeting all speaker needs from bookings to branding. Recruit renowned coaches. Develop digital systems managing operations remotely. Strategize diverse revenue models like subscription plans or affiliate incomes. Business ownership puts your leadership on worldwide display.

Critiquing and Improving Your Delivery

Perfecting delivery demands careful examination and refinement, which we'll explore through numerous coaching tools, video analysis techniques, and mock situation practices.

Working with a Speech Coach

Formally, coaching with a seasoned communications expert provides invaluable perspective and accountability. Qualified coaches will demonstrate techniques and deeply analyze strengths and areas needing work. When seeking a coach, inquire about credentials, specialties, and client successes. Signature coaching styles vary - some take directive roles while others facilitate self-discovery. Interview candidates to assess fit with your learning process. Develop rapport critical to growth with an aligned, patient mentor.

Applying Peer Feedback Mechanisms

Enlisting peers via structured feedback systems like "cold" reads injects objectivity. Groups such as Toastmasters provide platforms for rigorous peer review. Solicit peers through reciprocal agreements - you'll give thoughtful critiques of their speeches in exchange. Establish guidelines like focusing feedback on impact rather than personality. Note takeaways impartially for self-analysis. Peer perspectives supplement coach guidance, accelerating delivery mastery.

Using Video to Self-Critique

There is no better tool than video for objective delivery analysis. Record several practice runs on your phone to closely observe distinct aspects. Note physical mannerisms like fidgeting and pacing tendencies. Judge vocal attributes such as filler word volume fluctuations. Analyze style elements, including eye contact patterns and confidence projections. Study facial expressions and body language under pressure. Identify the most compelling versus stiff aspects for refinements. Repeat regularly tracking incremental improvements.

Diagramming Areas for Improvement

Map out specific factors needing work through organized reporting. Analyze critiques and videos strategizing incremental progress goals. Create a delivery tracking worksheet dividing physical, vocal, and style dimensions.

Record strengths and challenges within each category. Establish SMART goals prioritizing high-leverage fixes. Devise custom practice regimens addressing needs systematically. Revisit routinely monitoring accomplishments fueling motivation. Visual documentation speeds upgrades.

Practicing Vocal Variation

Mastering an expressive, dynamic speaking voice magnetizes listeners. Exercises vary in pitch, rate, tone, and volume, meaningfully punctuating ideas. Read aloud, deliberately alternating attributes between sentences. Gradually build speed by reciting favorite passages emphasizing distinct emotional qualities. Record yourself dissecting strong from flat delivery. Mimic acclaimed speakers trying new inflections. Repetition trains vocal dexterity, captivating any audience naturally.

Reducing Filler Words and Hesitations

Verbal pauses and placeholders like "um," "like," and "you know" diminish the impact. Identify and remove lingering habits through mindful practice. Analyze transcripts circling recurring placeholders. Read with provisions forbidding the crutches to temporarily stretch comfort. Reprogram pace and phrasing habits through mirror exercises, speaking as if recorded. Record to track progress - over time, new speech patterns will feel natural, conveying assuredness.

Refining Eye Contact Practices

Maintaining authentic, inclusive eye contact across audiences boosts rapport and authority. Develop techniques for scouting entire rooms comfortably. Start with close acquaintances practicing direct eye contact and marking key statements. Gradually shift focus systematically, scanning the full audience and repeating catchphrases. Videotape transitions identifying room coverage weaknesses. Devise strategic glance patterns welcoming all into the experience. Simulate larger crowds gaining poise.

Practicing with Props and Visuals

Reinforce major ideas through embodiment using demonstrative tools. Fine-tune natural interactions, enhancing comprehensibility. Select impactful props coordinated to distinct points. Practice smooth transitions, handling each with a carefree style. Gauge timing transitioning between discussion and visual references fluidly. Simulate technical difficulties by responding professionally. Record examining prop usage - adjust any aspects detracting from presence. Polish interactions until second nature.

Enhancing Facial Expressions

Varied, authentic facial expressions communicate empathy and animate delivery beyond words alone. Develop techniques for amplifying nonverbal storytelling. Study yourself in recordings labeling facial qualities dominating certain emotions. Map strategic smiling, eyebrow raises, and head tilts, punctuating key ideas. Practice amplifying affect through mirror work until instinctive. Record again carefully monitoring believable, consistent nonverbals, drawing listeners in viscerally.

Mastering Audience Interactions

Develop comfort in fielding questions confidently and leading crowd discussions eloquently. Practice thinking on your feet and maintaining control. Recruit question plants or hold mock Q&As. Hone listening skills like rephrasing queries and making eye contact. Develop composed, concise responses, avoiding rambling. Observe yourself handling pressure and redirecting interactions smoothly. Simulate distracting crowd behaviors, staying calm and in authority. Build improvisation dexterity through repetition.

Conducting Live Polls and Activities

Engage audiences directly through interactive techniques like live polling and games synchronizing with content. Develop flair, maintaining momentum. Brainstorm dynamic concepts matching points. Practice activity introductions, gaining instant participation. Develop questioning styles eliciting votes energetically yet methodically. Record leading several - note gestural guidance, keeping All attentive and syncing mobile responses quickly to retain flow. Fine-tune public facilitation abilities, instilling enjoyment.

Demonstrating Expertise Through Stories

Bring subjects to life, sharing true anecdotes demonstrating your authority. Develop memorable storytelling delivery showcasing charismatic speaking talents. Compile your most compelling experiences. Practice vocal techniques like pausing strategically. Develop characters vividly through descriptive gestures. Gage's emotional story arcs culminate in resolutions. The film has several telling analyzing narration flaws. Polish each story until you are transporting listeners intuitively to any place or time through your descriptions alone. Stories personalized eminence.

Practicing in Formal Business Attire

Presenting in typical business attire builds comfort when speaking professionally. Make wardrobe adjustments, maximizing composure. Rehearse major speeches dressed as if presenting to executives. Check tailored fit and accessorizing occupying attention or inhibiting natural arm/leg motions. Adjust perceived inhibitions. Assimilate nuanced power stances exuding authority regardless of dress. Attain assurance appearance aligns with the message without hindering delivery dynamics.

Mastering Live Session Introductions

Initial introductions set the stage compellingly. Hone introduction styles fit varied events, from conferences to small-scale talks. Craft sample introductions with varying formality, tone, and engagement tactics. Practice confident, composed delivery with diverse audiences in mind. Film introductions note elements rushing delivery or lacking vibrancy. Refine compelling pronunciation and gesturing, pulling others in immediately. Introductions deserve as much finesse as the speech itself.

Rehearsing in Actual Venues

Familiarize yourself with podiums, stages, seating arrangements, and audiovisuals to avoid jitters. Make pacing adjustments leveraging space dynamics. Schedule venue walkthroughs introducing yourself. Stand at lecterns practicing introductions under actual acoustic conditions and room sight lines. Note echoes or distracting backdrops. Gauge how speech variations carry, and eye contact patterns reach all areas. Customize planned movements mindful of surroundings to resonate wherever stationed. Territorial ownership translates to assured delivery.

PART 3

Real-World
Applications

CHAPTER 14

Public Speaking for Social Change

Advocating for Social and Environmental Causes

Advancing social justice and environmental protection starts with effective communication. This section focuses on how to craft and deliver impactful speeches that advocate for important causes.

Choosing the Right Cause

As discussed earlier, the first step is selecting an issue you feel passionately about. Research different causes to find one you truly care about and already have some knowledge of. Choose a narrow focus within that issue to target your advocacy. For example, rather than just "climate change," focus on a specific policy or initiative. Having a clearly defined goal helps guide your message.

The cause you choose must resonate deeply with you on a personal level. If you do not fully believe in and care about the issue, it will be difficult to communicate that passion and concern to others. You must feel motivated to dedicate serious time and effort towards achieving outcomes around this topic.

Framing the Problem Positively

When raising awareness of challenges, focus on optimistic framing over fear tactics. Explain why the issue matters - how it negatively impacts people's lives or society. Highlight moral or ethical reasons for action rather than doom and gloom. Give concrete examples to make abstract problems feel real and urgent without inducing panic or hopelessness.

It is important to connect the problem directly to people's lives and experiences. Use specific anecdotes that illustrate its personal consequences. However, take care to avoid graphic details that only evoke distress or discomfort without informing. Maintain a hopeful tone that motivates action.

Inspiring Hope Through Solutions

Do not just explain problems - propose realistic solutions. Give your audience an opportunity to support progress by getting involved. Offering tangible next steps like contacting representatives, volunteering, or donating empowers people to take positive action. Discuss current initiatives and successful models that give hope change is possible through a coordinated effort.

Well-researched solutions should address the root causes and offer a clear path forward. Recommendations must be politically and financially feasible while still effectively tackling the issue. Showing examples of programs that achieved change inspires confidence in your proposed solutions.

Connecting on an Emotional Level

Statistics lose impact over time. Instead of just numbers, connect issues to people through compelling personal stories. Hearing real human experiences makes advocacy feel less abstract and more emotionally engaging. Interview those impacted to share their journeys. However, get permission and avoid exploiting others' struggles without consent.

Personal testimonies from affected individuals help bring dry facts to life. Short anecdotes that highlight both challenges and hopes to resonate more than detached data. Respect, honor, and protect any individuals you feature by getting fully informed consent for their stories to be shared.

Calling the Audience to Action

Clearly state the specific call to action you want the audience to take at the conclusion. Give clear next steps like registering to vote, donating to an organization, or attending an upcoming rally people can easily act on. Reinforce why their participation matters and how even small actions contribute to larger goals when joined with others. Inspire audiences to continue involvement after the speech.

Provide audience members with any relevant supporting materials, like fact sheets, organization information, or contact details, to simplify following through on the next steps. Empower people by making it as easy as possible to get involved through minimally burdensome initial actions.

Adapting to Different Audiences

Messages must be tailored to specific groups. Learn the concerns, values, and interests of expected attendees to emphasize relevant impacts. Frame issues in bipartisan terms when possible. Some crowds cite faith-based rationales over economic ones. Test themes through practice presentations. Adjust content based on audience reactions to optimize persuasive impact.

Assessing the expected makeup and viewpoints of audiences allows for focusing on themes likely to resonate most. Pre-testing speeches in similar crowds provides feedback to enhance persuasiveness. Small changes targeting key interests can build deeper understanding across usual boundaries.

Addressing Objections and Skepticism

Anticipate potential concerns, counterarguments, or areas of doubt audiences may express. Directly acknowledge reasonable objections to diffuse criticism and build credibility. Research-based responses showing careful consideration of multiple perspectives reassure open-minded listeners. However, avoid getting bogged down in tangents that de-rail the overarching message.

Common objections like lack of political will, feasibility doubts, or skepticism of data should be addressed concisely with facts and rationale. Agreeing on shared goals like justice or future wellbeing can become common ground to build from despite minor technical disputes. The core values underneath surface disagreements usually align.

Calls to Perspective and Moral Responsibility

Some audiences need perspective shifts more than information. Frame issues through lenses of ethics, duty, and social justice. Cite philosophies and faith traditions emphasizing assistance, stewardship, and rights. Challenge cultural assumptions through respectful questioning. However, stay optimistic that positive change emerges as perspectives evolve on these foundations.

Appeals to Shared moral or religious values of duty, justice, and kindness can inspire action where rational self-interest alone does not. While social progress ideally comes through open-minded understanding, core principles of basic human welfare and rights provide compasses even where views differ. Collective responsibility and global citizenship support cooperative problem-solving.

The Science is Settled

For scientifically established issues, directly state key facts and refute myths to counter science denialism. Frame debates not as disputes requiring "balance" but as choices between knowledge and willful ignorance. However, avoid attacking opponents as much as winning them over through accessible scientific explanations. Unity, not division, serves advocacy goals.

Clear communication of politically neutral science for issues from vaccines to climate change strengthens cases where fear and falsehoods thrive. While denial cannot be directly debated, accessible presentations of predominant expert views inoculate open listeners against misinformation. However, inflammatory rhetoric only breeds further conflict, so patience remains key.

Calls for Justice and Values-Based Action

Some inequalities so contradict shared principles of fairness they require a forthright address. Explain how problems stem from systematic injustice or neglect of vulnerable communities. Appeal to higher principles like equality and dignity to inspire efforts advancing rights and inclusion. However, acknowledge the progress made and maintain hope where work remains.

For issues deeply entwined with justice, like poverty, discrimination, or lack of healthcare access, moral arguments grounded in civil and human rights especially motivate action. Call audiences to live up to stated democratic ideals through civic participation and allyship with marginalized communities. Focus on future goals of equality and community over past failures.

Coalition Building

Partnering with allied groups amplifies reach and presentation strength. Coordinate to discuss cross-cutting angles and divide content labor. Broader coalitions show a united front countering false "divide and conquer" narratives. Familiarize yourself with other organizations' priorities to reinforce natural linkages between causes like labor rights and environmental justice.

Cross-promotion exposes potential new allies to your mission and spurs action. For example, environmental non-profits gain members through labor coalition seminars stressing green jobs. In turn, those groups advertise conservation group volunteer occasions. Synergies arise where intersections exist between populations affected by interconnected issues.

Using Multimedia and Augmented Reality

Slides, videos, and interactive displays bring issues to life beyond speeches alone. Compelling photography and interview clips arouse empathy where mere descriptions fall flat. Location-based augmented reality exhibits also immerse audiences in cause-related experiences. However, ensure all media usage complies with copyright and respects the privacy of any individuals featured.

Short documentary previews profiling solutions models or directly affected people powerfully supplement speeches. For example, viewers touring an aquifer through virtual reality gain a new understanding of water protectors' perspectives. Multimedia adds dimensionality, lifting presentations beyond the basic informational level.

Incorporating Audience Feedback

Solicit questions and comments regularly to engage listeners actively. Invite members to discuss personal stakes in issues after initial presentations. Adjust future speeches based on shared perspectives, knowledge, and priorities surfaced. Dynamic discussions build long-term buy-in exceeding single-event impacts.

Respond respectfully to dissenting views as learning opportunities rather than threats. Thank all who contribute honestly to conversations, as varied input enhances advocacy. Follow-up by sharing how dialogue informed further efforts emphasizes commitment to the partnership over mere monologue.

Leveraging Community Connections

Establish yourself as a reliable neighborhood resource on target issues. Partner with local leaders and attend community spaces regularly to deepen trust over time. Whether discussing sustainability at the library or job equity concerns with labor unions, consistency shows investment beyond single speeches. Attendees eventually see you as an approachable expert.

Ask community partners how they think you could effectively support neighborhood efforts long-term. Sustainable advocacy requires listening humility to shape strategies cooperatively rather than solely through a singular agenda. Respectful relationships prove advocacy aims for assistance over personal gains.

Culturally Responsive Messaging

Recognize diverse audiences experience problems and priorities differently. Partner with cultural liaisons to learn language, traditions, and challenges facing marginalized ethnic or identity groups. Authentically addressing their specific stakes garners trust where outsiders normally fail. Translate key materials and find natural community Discussion forums to disseminate information through organic circles.

For example, health issues disproportionately impacting indigenous communities require examining blame-focused narratives and instead advocating systematic changes addressing root socioeconomic factors. Respect requires actively learning cultural nuances and following group guidance over outside assumptions.

Grassroots Organizing Basics

Explain how speaking at relevant neighborhood meetings espouses issues. Recruit volunteers to canvass their zip codes, connecting personally with others motivated locally. Support letter-writing or call campaigns petitioning representatives. Promote upcoming lobbying days with transportation. Consistency in these scattered interpersonal interactions builds widespread advocacy bases.

Successful movements utilize diverse tactics cumulatively, pressuring institutions systematically. No single strategy prevails alone - only coordinated complementarity achieves change. Maintaining group chat threads organizes these dispersed conversations under overarching campaigns. Synergy arises when individual actions link into unified movements.

Activism through Public Speaking

Once an issue is chosen, public speaking can help spread awareness, recruit supporters, and further activism on college campuses and in local communities. Speeches combine with other strategies for maximum impact on pressing challenges.

Recruiting Volunteers

As mentioned earlier, effectively appeal to volunteers by clearly defining tasks requiring various time commitments people can choose from. Stories from current members help others picture themselves also helping. Follow up promptly with interested contacts to turn interest into action.

Provide point persons for common onboarding queries so new volunteers feel supported. Introduce recruits into uplifting activist communities where their contributions feel valued alongside others'. Ongoing appreciation and feedback sustain involvement exceeding single events.

Promoting Events

Build excitement for rallies, walks, and other functions by detailing logistics alongside motivations to attend. Highlight influential speakers or activities resonating with subgroups. Distribute eye-catching promotional materials through speech networks.

Creative outreach leveraging multimedia generates buzz exceeding posters alone. Prominently feature community partners assisting with event planning to recognize their efforts. Update audiences after with recaps emphasizing impacts made through collaboration.

Fundraising Strategies

Explain budgets and tangible impacts donations enable. Provide promotional materials, campaign collateral, and donation forms for direct contributions. Connect pitches to broader crowdfunding benefiting the cause long-term. Thank all donors publicly. Donation campaigns unite financial support with dedicated activism. Thanking various gift levels equally creates inclusive movement cultures. Distributing donor acknowledgments during follow-ups recognizes continued involvement as valuable as singular donations.

Coalition Building

As mentioned earlier, partnering with allied causes amplifies messaging by merging under shared themes. Coordinate with groups representing diverse backgrounds for maximum cooperative impact. Cross-promotion introduces audiences one organization may not reach to both groups' aligned missions. United front's counteract narratives of division among communities advocating justice on interconnected issues. Combining strengths leverages change beyond any single entity's capacity alone.

Community Organizing

Clearly present specific policy actions for engaged residents. Provide templates empowering people to directly pressure decision-makers through accessible modalities. Build momentum by encouraging involvement through escalating tactics.

Directly involving community stakeholders transforms them from passive observers to invested campaign leaders. Localizing regional or national issues empowers grassroots participants, driving hypervisor change from the bottom up.

Campus Activism

As stated earlier, impactful presentations recruit new members and propose experiential learning opportunities. Guest lectures mobilize behind campus issues. Collaborate offering applied public speech roles furthering coordinated campaigns. Academic partnerships strengthen intergenerational movement building. By spotlighting student voices through tailored programming, movements showcase future leadership while appealing to youth demographics. Knowledge disseminates organically across social circles.

Coalition Infrastructure

Establish guidelines outlining clear responsibilities, expectations, communication protocols, and decision-making processes for collaborative bodies. Rotate convening responsibilities to distribute labor. United fronts survive long-term through formalizing equitable ground rules, maintaining transparency, accountability, and consensus-based work.

However, flexible structures adapt organically according to emergent priorities over rigid bureaucracy.

Leadership Development

Intentional mentorship cultivates future advocates. Guide interested volunteers navigating public roles with grading assistance. Promote qualified partners to panelists or organize positions matching their skills and ambitions. Growth arises through guided participation exceeding passive membership. Uplifting new leaders sustainably and passing on accumulated wisdom ensures movements outlive original founders. Intergenerational support catalyzes long-term social change.

Strategic Campaign Planning

Coordinate short and long-term objectives, target outcomes, resource needs, and timed tactics into blueprints to maximize impact. Review analyses and update plans regularly per shift. Holistic strategies linking complementary activities materialize visions for change exceeding piecemeal reactions. Consistent evaluation and recalibration maintain dynamism, whereas stagnation decreases effectiveness. Shared problem-solving cultivates investment and buy-in.

Self-Care and Sustaining Momentum

Promote practices sustaining members' physical, emotional, and spiritual health, avoiding burnout. Offer wellness resources and encourage time-off without guilt. Celebrate incremental achievements, boosting morale. Movements outlive challenges alone through caring for the whole humans within them. Appreciating one another as multi-dimensional beings beyond singular roles models balanced, restorative justice-centered approaches essential to long campaigns. Revitalization replenishes endurance, driving victories.

Messaging and Media Relations

Craft clear advocacy narratives digestible to diverse crowds. Prioritize accessibility over inside jargon. Prepare spokespeople skilled in presenting complexities concisely to reporters. Relatable storytelling builds understanding beyond factions. Proactive media engagement frames coverage, countering misrepresentations threatening momentum. Correcting misconceptions maintains credibility.

Social Media Strategizing

Coordinate online campaigns spreading awareness. Train members utilizing optimized hashtags to broaden reach. Leverage visual storytelling showcasing realities beyond text alone. Analyze engagement, boosting future tactics.

Strategic digital organizing organically exposes causes to untapped audiences. Data-driven improvements maximize impacts. User-generated content deepens relating beyond stale templates. Creative efforts inspire the sharing of information virally.

Direct Action Techniques

Explain dignified protest roles respecting diverse comfort levels. Suggest appropriately permitted rallies, sit-ins, or marches for various involvement stages. Provide legal observing or rapid response team training.

Peaceful demonstrations effectively apply political pressure beyond solely online clicks. Guidance empowers participants to exercise their rights to assemble and petition authorities. Understanding protections and proper conduct cultivates effectiveness beyond catharsis.

Policy Campaign Tactics

Outline legislative or bureaucratic targets. Propose template emails, telephone scripts, or postcards en masse notifying representatives of constituent priorities. Schedule lobbying days transporting pre-briefed delegations.

Direct civic engagement compels systemic reforms to exceed surface-level transformations. Grassroots lobbying counters moneyed interests through coordinated numbers. Training ensures clarity and confidence, maximizing access to decision-makers.

Beyond Binding Arbitration

Suggest respectful yet unrelenting pressure modalities, including nonviolent direct action when responsive policy changes fail to materialize. Emphasize perseverance through various tactics united towards a shared long-term vision for justice and healing.

Transformation arises gradually through diverse avenues simultaneously applied. Setbacks strengthen commitments to alternates challenging underlying structures sustaining harms. Nonviolence and truth weather opposition, inviting redemption where aggression breeds further conflict.

Cross-Sector Partnerships

Collaborate with allied groups across sectors. For example, link labor activists advocating exclusion policies with environmentalists concerned about poor neighborhoods' pollution burdens. Amplify shared stances empowering diverse constituencies.

Progress advances most sustainably through intersectional cooperation counteracting "broken windows" mentalities. By recognizing intertwined oppressions, no community faces alone and uniting toward comprehensive freedom, movements redistributing political power emerge.

Grassroots-Professional Synergy

Tap volunteer energies alongside experienced campaign strategists. Provide supporters guidance amplifying skills through organized civic participation. However, center movement leadership within directly impacted groups.

Accountability necessitates guarding against co-optation, yet effectiveness integrates accumulated expertise, elevating lived experiences. Equity requires responsible allocation of accumulated privilege investing in others' self-determination. Liberation arises through cooperation but never alone.

Meshing Online and Offline Tactics

Integrate on-the-ground organizing with strategic digital presences. Host webinars are inviting geographically dispersed allies into local seminars. Stream rallies engaging broader public support networks.

Blended virtual-physical synergies multiply footprints. While technology connects far-flung supporters, nothing replaces face-to-face community-building, cementing movements. Complementary strengths surmount online tactics' limitations and offline tactics' insularity.

Self-Determination and Allyship

Amplify leadership of most impacted groups, centering their expertise. Provide support requested respecting autonomous decision-making. Combat tendencies are treating solidarity as a solution alone through education emphasizing systemic transformation responsibilities.

True justice emerges through those most burdened determining solutions addressing their needs - not outsider savior mentalities. At the same time, allies question blind spots; liberation remains not a gift but a right. Movements model new societies, elevating marginalized voices above comfortable noises.

Navigating Controversial Topics

While challenging issues motivate speakers, navigating opposition skillfully remains crucial. Nuanced discussions require deftly managing emotions and dissenting perspectives.

Anticipating Counterarguments

As mentioned earlier, effectively prepare by researching weaknesses skeptics may raise to develop rebuttals. Address dissenting views upfront to show consideration and diffuse unintended opposition. Conceding minor points where reasonable build ethos.

Imagining alternative viewpoints strengthens advocating one's own position. However, acknowledging the reality that some dissent originates less from reason than from biases challenging is uncomfortable. Patience and understanding remain key to eventual persuasion where possible.

Reframing Polarized Debates

Explore bipartisan facets and shared democratic principles whenever possible to appeal across boundaries. Find common goals like justice and equality where disagreements seem inevitable. Such ground restores civility were confrontation risks escalation.

While acknowledging integrity in disagreements, focus on outcomes serving humanity over tribalism. Appeal to our strongest principles of compassion, resisting none's dehumanization. Where justice aligns all, understanding motivates action were condemnation breeds defensiveness.

Managing Heated Questions

As stated earlier, deescalate hostility by restating positions clearly and concisely without provocation. Redirect aggressors to discussing solutions jointly serving the public good through open-minded problem-solving. Maintain respectful conclusions, allowing space for further growth.

Leading by EXAMPLE, welcome challenges as learning facilitating empathy over escalation. Recenter discussions on shared hopes for the community when disagreements arise and criticism turns toxic. Nonviolence overcomes violence's temporary victories with permanent social evolution.

Overcoming Discomfort Around Disagreement

As mentioned previously, controversies understandably trigger emotions requiring preparation. However, recall leaders are facilitating progress through steadfast nonviolence. Have allies strategize likely objections to lessen unease. Courteous conviction strengthens advocacy where intimidation risks derailing messages.

The discomfort signals growth opportunities - not failure. With practice, skill in respectfully listening as much as in speaking develops. And with open ears attuned to others' humanity comes confidence that truth and reconciliation strengthen where conflict divides. Progress lies in continuing difficult conversations, not avoiding them.

Clarifying Misconceptions Respectfully

Gently correct factually inaccurate claims by appealing to objectively verifiable evidence. Frame disputes not as attacks but as chances for shared enlightenment. Thank skeptics for perspectives while restating facts to inform without accusation.

Understanding prevents as much as correcting. Asking for clarification models learning from others - not debating them. And opening previously closed perspectives lifts all seekers of truth, however belatedly they arrive. Humility and care in dialogue foster understanding where defensiveness breeds further conflict.

Conceding Legitimate Critiques

Acknowledge reasonable objections to one's own position, demonstrating intellectual honesty. Admitting imperfect knowledge merits respect exceeding the pretense of infallibility. However, qualified concessions do not invalidate movement goals but respect dissent's legitimacy.

Ownership of limitations invites partnership through humility. And partnership strengthens causes more through appreciation of shared hopes than through resentment of differences. Progress lies in continually refining stances - not clinging to past arguments beyond reason's evolution.

Developing allyship with Critics

Seek common ground with even skeptics - not just agreement. Thank dissenters also for honest participation and elevating discussions. Find allies wherever understanding and justice align, though views diverge elsewhere.

Listening changes more minds than lecturing. And minds changed through willfulness become convictions - while minds changed by persuasion seeds further thought. Together, gradually separating personhood from position, understanding emerges where debate once reigned.

Reframing "Two Sides" Fallacies

Challenge false dichotomies of "two equal perspectives" on asymmetrical issues of harm. Cite power dynamics and consequences of inaction. However, condemning acts - not persons - as becoming justice requires convicted nonviolence overreaction.

Complexities exist beyond oversimplified binaries. But neutrality serves only the status quo of injustice when rights are systematically denied. Truth invites society toward equity and restoration - not accusation. And restoration heals where accusation divides.

Addressing Science Denialism

As stated earlier, directly share key facts countering myths when scientifically verifiable harms are falsely equated with responsible concerns. Translate prevalent expertise into accessible languages, disempowering misinformation where fears facilitate detachment from reality.

However, condemnation converts few. With patience, compassion, and leading by promoting understanding, confirmation biases relax their grip. Affirming our shared hopes and emphasizing cooperation over conflict cultivates thinking partners from those initially disagreeing.

Values-Based Persuasion

As mentioned previously, some debates shift less through information exchange than by reframing issues according to ethics and justice principles audiences affirm. Appeal to shared hopes inspiring action where facts alone fail to motivate. Stay solution-oriented, maintaining hope in humanity's moral evolution.

Progress emerges gradually as perspectives broaden to encompass others. Conviction arises from conscience, not coercion alone. And conscience seeks truth through understanding, not victories. Together, step by step, awareness grows where forced agreement remains elusive. But growing together moves farther than arguing apart.

Addressing Emotional Reactions Respectfully

Some discussions trigger deep-seated fears or anger, requiring acknowledging emotions respectfully. Validate discomfort caused by confronting hard truths while avoiding defensiveness. Offer tissue or breaks as needed with compassion.

Connection, not division, facilitates insight. With care and patience, perspectives shift as shared vulnerabilities emerge from initial defensiveness. Reframe debates as opportunities for healing where understanding emerges from honesty navigated nonviolently.

Reframing Social Injustices Systemically

Contextualize controversial topics systemically countering reduction to isolated acts. Explain how power structures and cultural conditioning sustain wider inequalities where direct victims receive blame alone. Appeal to conscience over the accusation.

Justice rests on dismantling underlying oppression, not punishing individuals whose harmful actions often reflect subconscious socializations. By recognizing intersectional marginalization's no community experiences alone, understanding replaces defensiveness in even difficult exchanges.

Clarifying Misunderstandings Humbly

Gently acknowledge discontinuity between intentions and impacts, allowing critics opportunities to refine perspectives charitably. Do not deflect responsibility, but express openness to humanity's fallibility with patience.

Humility and care invite not defensiveness but thoughtfulness. And thoughtfulness born of understanding moves closer to truth than stances held rigidly. Progress emerges through partners committed to continually refining views - not through proselytization alone.

Affirming Shared Values

Refocus debates onto likenesses underneath disagreements by emphasizing justice and dignity principles affirming audiences. Appeal to conscience over reaction, inviting consideration through empathy instead of attacks.

Connections formed through shared hopes empower discussions where defensiveness is disabled. Focusing on the direction toward equity over stances keeps dialogues constructive. And construction builds understanding, where destruction breeds further conflict.

Practicing Nonviolence in Speech

Avoid claims targeting persons - only harmful acts or systems. Do not escalate tension through provocation, but reduce heat with patience. Defuse hostility through reason and care for humanity, even opponents.

Leading by example, welcome criticisms without resentment. And resentment dissolved leads toward partners in progress - where it gives fuel only for further conflict. Nonviolence conquers through persuasion, not domination. Persuasion respects each mind's autonomy equally under justice.

Affirming Citizens' Shared Interests

Find positives even in critiques as contributions to collectively discerning truth. Thank questioners and emphasize shared hopes over differences. Remind audiences of interdependence - our societies rise and fall together beyond surface disagreements.

Connection forms the basis for understanding, whereas division enables only conflict, prolonging injustice. By appealing to our universal stake in the community, discussions lift all and invite reconsidering positions that divide what shares a common fate. From interdependence comes insight transcending reaction.

Exercising Patience and Humility

Understanding perspectives evolves gradually through experience. Do not expect opponents to instantly alter entrenched worldviews challenged - but plant seeds for future growth. And grow together through questions asked and answered with care.

Humility remains the surest guide into controversies' complexities. Patience is the steadiest walk, emerging with understanding intact where haste risks derailing. Insight comes not as an arrival but as a journey - not a possession but a relationship. Such journeys sustain long after speeches end.

Personal Growth through Dialogue

Admit limitations and acknowledge lessons learned from discussions navigated earnestly. Thank questioners for expanding perspectives through respectful inquiry. Commit to ongoing learning alongside former dissenters.

The open exchange becomes not a battle but a partnership when all embark on learning. From shared discovery comes shared understanding - and understanding transforms conflict into cooperation. Journeying together toward fuller insights lifts all ahead of were arguing alone could take.

The Bravery of Civil Discourse

Addressing conflict civilly despite emotional triggers demands moral courage. However, nonviolence overcomes through patience what confrontation achieves temporarily. Have faith that truth and reconciliation gain permanent victories where escalation sows only seeded conflict. Stay determined yet calm.

Bravery resides not in domination but in empowering understanding through respect. And respect pioneers' progress by inviting reconsideration patiently - not reaction. With care and unshakeable commitment to justice, controversial discussions move all nearer solutions division forestalls.

CHAPTER 15

International and Cross-Cultural Communication

Speaking in Multilingual and Multicultural Settings

In our increasingly globalized world, it's essential to be able to speak in settings where multiple languages and cultures converge. Whether you're delivering a presentation to an international business audience, participating in a multilingual conference, or addressing a diverse community event, the ability to navigate multilingual and multicultural settings is a valuable skill. This section will delve into the challenges and opportunities of speaking in such environments, providing insights and strategies to help you succeed.

Understanding Language Diversity:

Language diversity is a hallmark of multilingual and multicultural settings. It's not uncommon to encounter audiences with various mother tongues, making it crucial to have a fundamental understanding of this diversity. The challenge often lies in the fact that not everyone in the audience may be fluent in the language you're speaking. This necessitates the use of interpreters, the incorporation of translation tools, or even the inclusion of multiple languages in your speech.

To successfully address language diversity, consider the use of interpreters. Professional interpreters can bridge the language gap, ensuring that your message is accurately conveyed to a multilingual audience. It's essential to work closely with interpreters, providing them with your speech in advance to ensure they are well-prepared. Additionally, being mindful of pacing and allowing pauses for interpretation can enhance comprehension. When incorporating multiple languages into your speech, do so strategically. Ensure that it aligns with the context and interests of your audience. For example, use the local language when addressing a community event or utilize a lingua franca when speaking to an international audience.

Adapting Your Speech Style:

When speaking in multilingual and multicultural settings, it's crucial to adapt your speech style to accommodate a diverse audience. Recognize that different languages and cultures have unique communication styles and expectations. This is not only about using the correct words but also about how you deliver them. The tone, pace, and even the use of idiomatic expressions can impact the effectiveness of your communication.

To adapt your speech style effectively, start by researching your audience's preferences. Understanding their communication style is key to connecting with them. For instance, some cultures may value a more direct and concise communication style, while others may appreciate more elaborate and metaphorical language. Adapting your tone and pace is equally important. Speaking too quickly may leave non-native speakers struggling to keep up, while speaking too slowly might bore the fluent speakers. Strive to find a balance that accommodates both groups.

Incorporating Visual Aids:

Visual aids can be indispensable in multilingual and multicultural settings. They provide a visual context that can enhance comprehension, especially when language alone may not suffice. Incorporating visuals effectively means choosing the right images, diagrams, or multimedia presentations that align with your message and resonate with your diverse audience.

Effective use of visual aids begins with selecting images that are universal in meaning and don't rely on language. Infographics, charts, and diagrams can often transcend linguistic barriers, making complex information more accessible. However, ensure that visuals are culturally sensitive. What might be perfectly acceptable in one culture may be offensive in another. Take the time to research and understand the cultural connotations of the visuals you plan to use. Additionally, if you use slides, keep them uncluttered and concise. Excessive text or information can overwhelm your audience.

Using Nonverbal Communication:

Nonverbal communication is a universal language that transcends linguistic and cultural boundaries. In multilingual and multicultural settings, the effective use of nonverbal cues becomes particularly important. Your body language, facial expressions, and gestures can convey meaning, emotion, and intent, even when words are not readily understood.

Harnessing nonverbal communication starts with being mindful of your own body language. Maintain an open and confident posture, make eye contact, and use expressive facial expressions that match the tone of your message. Gestures can also be a powerful tool, but they should be used with caution. Some gestures have different meanings in different cultures, so it's essential to research and be aware of these potential pitfalls. In some cases, it might be more effective to use universally understood gestures, such as a thumbs-up or a nod of approval, to ensure your message is clear and well-received.

Dealing with Language Barriers:

Language barriers can be a significant challenge when speaking in multilingual and multicultural settings. They have the potential to create misunderstandings and disengage your audience. However, with the right strategies, you can effectively address and overcome these barriers, ensuring that your message is well-received by everyone present.

To address language barriers, consider simplifying your language. Choose straightforward and clear expressions over complex vocabulary. Avoid jargon, idiomatic phrases, or colloquialisms that may not be universally understood. It's also helpful to use visual cues to support your verbal message. For example, you can use props, gestures, or images that align with your content. This provides additional context and aids comprehension.

Pre-event communication is another key strategy. Reach out to your audience in advance to understand their language preferences and needs. This can help you tailor your presentation accordingly. Moreover, consider providing written materials, like a summary or transcript of your speech, in multiple languages. This allows the audience to follow along and review the content at their own pace, reinforcing their understanding.

Building Language Skills:

If you anticipate speaking frequently in multilingual settings, investing in language skills can be a game-changer. While becoming fluent in multiple languages is a substantial commitment, acquiring basic proficiency and learning key phrases and expressions can significantly enhance your effectiveness as a speaker in diverse environments.

Developing language skills can start with online courses, language apps, or local language classes. Focus on learning essential phrases and greetings, as well as common expressions related to your field or topic. Practicing pronunciation is equally important. Engaging in conversation with native speakers can provide valuable insights and boost your confidence. Moreover, embrace the power of language learning communities and resources available online, where you can find language partners and practice with native speakers.

Understanding Cultural Nuances

Cultural nuances are a significant factor when communicating with diverse audiences. Ignoring or misunderstanding these subtleties can lead to miscommunication, offense, or an ineffective presentation. This section will guide you through understanding and respecting cultural nuances, ensuring your message is well-received and culturally sensitive.

Cultural Awareness

Cultural awareness is the foundation of understanding and respecting cultural nuances. It involves developing an appreciation for the customs, values, and traditions of the cultures you're addressing. To achieve this, research is your best ally. Familiarize yourself with your target audience's history, social norms, and cultural values. Understand their festivals, rituals, and significant historical events. The more you know about the culture, the better you can tailor your message and delivery to resonate with your audience.

An excellent practice is engaging with members of the culture in advance, either through personal interviews, surveys, or networking with individuals with experience in that culture. This firsthand insight can provide valuable information beyond what is available in books or online resources. Furthermore, it showcases your genuine interest in understanding and respecting the culture, which your audience can appreciate.

Cultural Appropriateness

While cultural awareness is the first step, it's equally important to assess the cultural appropriateness of your content and approach. What may be perfectly acceptable in one culture could be deemed offensive or inappropriate in another. Therefore, it's essential to review your content, stories, and examples from the lens of cultural appropriateness.

For instance, consider the use of Humor. Jokes and anecdotes that are well-received in one culture may fall flat or even offend in another. Stereotypes and clichés should also be avoided. These oversimplified portrayals can perpetuate biases and negatively impact your audience's perception of your message.

When assessing cultural appropriateness, it's beneficial to consult with individuals from the culture you're addressing or experts in intercultural communication. They can provide invaluable feedback and guidance, helping you navigate potential pitfalls and refine your approach to align with the cultural sensibilities of your audience.

Respecting Local Customs

Consider incorporating or acknowledging local customs and traditions into your speech to create a positive and lasting impression on your multicultural audience. This demonstrates respect and an effort to connect with the culture personally.

One way to respect local customs is to begin your presentation with a gesture of goodwill. For example, if you're addressing an audience in a culture where bowing is customary, consider a respectful bow a sign of acknowledgment and appreciation. If you're speaking at a cultural event or festival, be prepared to participate in the rituals or ceremonies, showing that you're not merely a spectator but an active and respectful participant.

Additionally, you can weave local anecdotes or references into your speech. This makes your message more relatable and resonant with the audience. Sharing stories or examples that draw from the culture's history or achievements can help you establish a deeper connection and build rapport.

Adapting Your Content

Adapting your content to your audience's cultural preferences and values is essential for effective cross-cultural communication. This involves tailoring your speech, stories, and examples to resonate with a particular cultural group.

Start by understanding the core values of the culture you're addressing. Some cultures place a high value on community and collectivism, while others emphasize individualism and personal achievement. You can reflect these values in your content. For instance, speaking to a collectivist culture focuses on the benefits of collaboration and community, whereas in an individualistic culture, you might emphasize personal success and achievement.

Moreover, consider the cultural context of your speech. Can you connect specific cultural touchpoints or historical events with your message? Finding common ground between your topic and the culture can make your speech more relatable and engaging.

Cultural Sensitivity in Visuals

Visuals, including images and slides, can convey cultural insensitivity if not chosen carefully. What may seem innocuous in one culture can be offensive or misunderstood in another. Therefore, it's vital to select visuals that are universally understood and culturally sensitive.

When choosing visuals, aim for images and graphics with broad cross-cultural appeal. Steer clear of images that may be linked to stereotypes, biases, or cultural insensitivity. For example, images depicting individuals in traditional dress engaged in everyday activities or celebrating culturally significant events are often well-received.

If you're uncertain about the cultural sensitivity of certain visuals, seek feedback from individuals from that culture or experts in cross-cultural communication. They can help you identify potential issues and suggest alternative visuals that align with the culture's values and sensibilities.

Navigating Taboos and Sensitive Topics

Some topics may be sensitive or taboo in certain cultures and addressing them without caution can lead to discomfort or offense among your audience. Being aware of these topics and navigating them sensitively is vital when speaking in multicultural settings.

Before your presentation, conduct thorough research to identify sensitive topics or taboos within the culture you're addressing. These can vary widely from culture to culture and may include discussions related to religion, politics, social issues, or historical events. Once identified, make a conscious effort to avoid these topics or address them with extreme care.

If a sensitive topic is integral to your speech, consider prefacing it with a disclaimer acknowledging the sensitivity and your intention to discuss it respectfully and with an open mind. Additionally, engage with local experts or individuals from the culture to gain insights into how best to approach these subjects. Being transparent and open to discussion can help mitigate potential negative reactions and demonstrate your commitment to cultural sensitivity.

Building Global Connections through Public Speaking

Public speaking has the power to transcend borders and cultures, making it an indispensable tool for building global connections. Whether you're an international diplomat, a business leader, or a passionate advocate for change, your ability to communicate effectively can shape the course of events globally.

Cultural Diplomacy

Cultural diplomacy through public speaking is a subtle yet profound way to represent your culture and promote mutual respect between nations and societies. When you take the stage as an ambassador of your culture, you're not just delivering a speech; you're creating an opportunity for your audience to engage with a world they might not be familiar with. This is especially significant in today's globalized world, where cultures intertwine and intermingle like never before. You can break down stereotypes and foster appreciation by demonstrating your culture's richness, values, and contributions. Public speaking allows you to showcase the cultural tapestry of your nation, building bridges that transcend political boundaries. Through your words and actions, you can inspire curiosity and respect, encouraging others to explore and understand your culture more deeply. The impact of cultural diplomacy can ripple through generations, leading to better international relations, increased tourism, and enriched cultural exchanges.

Networking and Relationship Building

Public speaking is a powerful platform for networking and global relationship-building. Whether delivering a keynote at an international conference or addressing a diverse audience at a cultural event, you can connect with individuals and organizations from different backgrounds. Your connections through public speaking can lead to collaborations, partnerships, and opportunities that may not have arisen otherwise. Networking is more than just collecting business cards; it's about creating meaningful relationships to drive positive change. When you address an international audience, you open doors to a world of possibilities.

Promoting Global Causes

Public speaking can be a force for good, especially when promoting global causes. Whether you advocate for environmental conservation, social justice, or public health, your words can reach a global audience and ignite positive change. Your message can transcend borders, inspiring individuals from different cultures to unite in a common cause. When you take the stage to champion a global issue, you become a voice for those who might not have the platform or opportunity to speak for themselves. Your speech can raise awareness, mobilize support, and push for policy changes on an international scale. By crafting and delivering your message skillfully, you can inspire action, spark grassroots movements, and engage individuals and organizations worldwide. Public speaking allows you to amplify your message and make a genuine impact on issues that matter to both your local and global communities.

International Collaborations

Public speaking can lead to exciting international collaborations. As you engage with diverse audiences, you will likely encounter individuals, organizations, and institutions that share your passion or vision. These encounters can blossom into partnerships that transcend geographical boundaries. Whether in academia, business, or the nonprofit sector, the connections you make through public speaking can pave the way for joint initiatives, research projects, and business ventures with a global reach. International collaborations can result in a synergistic exchange of ideas and resources, ultimately contributing to innovative solutions and addressing complex global challenges. Moreover, working with partners from different cultural backgrounds can provide fresh perspectives and diverse approaches, enriching the quality of your projects and broadening your worldview. Public speaking is the starting point for these connections, and it's up to you to nurture and develop them into meaningful and fruitful collaborations.

Cross-Cultural Empathy

Building global connections necessitates a deep understanding of cross-cultural empathy. Public speaking can play a vital role in developing this skill. When you address audiences from various cultural backgrounds, you can immerse yourself in their perspectives, values, and concerns. This immersion fosters empathy, enabling you to relate to people from different walks of life and appreciate their unique experiences. Cross-cultural empathy is not merely an understanding of differences; it's the ability to feel and connect with individuals on a human level, transcending cultural boundaries. This empathy can lead to more profound relationships, greater collaboration, and the ability to bridge divides. As a public speaker, you can use your platform to encourage others to develop this essential skill, promoting a more empathetic and interconnected world. Cross-cultural empathy is a two-way street, and by fostering it, you contribute to a more harmonious global society where diversity is celebrated rather than a source of division.

Global Impact

In an age of digital connectivity, the impact of public speaking can extend far beyond the physical stage. Your speeches can reach a global audience through online platforms, social media, and streaming services. This expanded reach allows you to influence individuals and communities worldwide, making your words potent for global impact. By utilizing technology and social media, you can measure and maximize the reach of your message, tracking engagement, feedback, and audience demographics. This data can help you refine your approach and tailor your content to resonate with global audiences better.

Furthermore, public speaking can inspire others to act and create a ripple effect as your audience shares your message with their networks. The potential for global impact is substantial, and it's a testament to the enduring power of words to shape opinions, change behaviors, and drive positive change on a global scale. Your speeches can catalyze a better, more connected world where ideas and cultures converge, enriching our collective human experience.

Conclusion

We have covered an immense amount of territory on this journey together. From uncovering the initial seeds of self-doubt to harvesting the ripe fruits of eloquent delivery, you now possess so many of the tools needed to step fully into your power as an impactful public speaker.

Yet mastery is not about perfection in a final moment of glory but an ongoing evolution over a lifetime. The great speakers understand their voices continue to develop across years and decades. However, what marks their success is not waiting until some fabled end-point to begin having influence. So as you round this bend in your development and look ahead to new vistas of opportunity, never forget that your distinctive, needed voice is prepared right now to create change.

I have been honored to provide maps, companionship and support as your guide, but the actual trailblazing has come through your courage and persistence alone. The terrain at the start looked so formidable, but in facing what felt insurmountable, through small steps of progress, you have ascended heights once unimaginable. And now as you survey your new view, take pride in just how far you have come.

Yet this is no place to build monuments or even rest for long. As we know, true success comes not from accolades delivered at destinations but through the empowerment we feel while moving purposefully towards them. And it is time now to define what those next horizons will be for you, personally, as a public speaker.

What pulsing social needs or injustices cry out to be spoken to through your unique voice and platform? What communities or institutions could be set on a better path with the perspectives your words can provide? What emerging audiences need exactly the story you alone can share?

The reach and accessibility of online media has dismantled so many of the old gatekeepers, allowing fresh ideas to spread through networks organically, powered by conviction alone. And remember that sparks need not roar like wildfire to set change in motion. Even the smallest flame can illuminate and warm if tended carefully. Not every speech needs to rival Hamlet's soliloquy in lyrical intensity or King's 'I Have a Dream' address in historical sweep to have intense meaning. Simple stories bravely told about injustices experienced or policy failings observed can acquiesce isolated minds while fortifying the resolve of allies. On issues of ethics, empathy and human dignity we each carry inside us powerful tales awaiting vocalization.

Of course, not all that yearns to be spoken should always be broadcast openly in raw form immediately. Wisdom comes in discerning which ideas have been adequately nurtured and are aligned with both greater truth as well as current audience needs. Here is where trusted mentors play such a pivotal role, helping us refine sensitive messages and find the appropriate venues for their delivery. We all gain deeper insight too from carefully studying great social movement orators across history. Note both the substance and structure of their addresses. Observe sequence, tone and technique. Continuously evaluate your own growing craft against the finest examples.

The pages of this book merely mark a commencement, not a culmination. While equipped now with so many empowering skills, speech making remains an ongoing apprenticeship as the ever-changing dynamics of audiences, media technologies and language itself continuously remake the landscape. Thus staying open and humble to new learning opportunities elevates the lifelong speaker. Perhaps the greatest myth to avoid is that a point ever exists where one's voice is so complete, original or authoritative that it requires no further refinement, skill strengthening or diversifying. Great public voices across eras understand they always stand on the shoulders of teachers and schools of thought who enabled their voices to first flower. Pay that gift forward by mentoring others now working to articulate their untapped power.

Finally, while boldness and conviction are virtues in voicing change, so too are patience, compassion and wisdom. Not all resistance we encounter while speaking out emanates from malign sources. Consider deeply too the hearts and minds of those unmoved by your speech. Identify real roots of skepticism rather than assume malice. With empathy, areas of alignment often emerge allowing progress. And where genuine disagreements remain, retain enough humility to admit fallibility in your own views. Our collective understanding continually unfolds through respectful civil dialogue. Perhaps the most lasting impact comes not from haranguing the hesitant into compliance but dialogue and leading by ethical example.

So venture forth now my friends, empowered, heartened and connected to the global chorus rising in hopeful unison through speech that enlightens, inspires and transforms. Lift all boats with the righteous tide of your voice. I sail alongside you in solidarity. Now speak your truth with courage! The world is ready at last to hear it.

Made in the USA
Monee, IL
24 June 2024

60451100R00089